D0266341

NEWI Information and Student Services
To renew a book ring the helpdesk
01978 293237

THE BURLESQUE TRADITION
IN THE ENGLISH THEATRE
AFTER 1660

HEROIC DECLAMATION

Mrs. Liston in the part of Queen Dollalolla

From an etching by George Cruikshank

THE BURLESQUE TRADITION IN THE ENGLISH THEATRE AFTER 1660

By

V. C. CLINTON-BADDELEY

With thirteen half-tone plates

LONDON
METHUEN & CO LTD
BARNES & NOBLE BOOKS
NEW YORK

First published in 1952
This edition reprinted 1973 by
Methuen & Co Ltd
11 New Fetter Lane
London EC4P 4EE
and Barnes & Noble Books, New York
10 East 53rd Street
New York NY 10022
(a division of Harper & Row Inc.)
Printed in Great Britain by
Whitstable Litho, Straker Brothers Ltd

Methuen SBN 416 79010 0
Barnes & Noble SBN 06 471235 4

"I believe the glory of sporting with sacred things
is peculiar to the English Nation"

JOHN WESLEY, *June 26, 1738.*

PREFACE

ON December 31, 1926, my adaptation of *Behind The Beyond* by
Stephen Leacock was unexpectedly translated from the stage of
the Cambridge A.D.C. to the St. Martin's Theatre, London,
where it was played as a curtain-raiser during the last months
of the run of *Berkeley Square*. This led me to dramatize three
more Leacock stories, and then to think about printing them
with a long preface on the history and traditions of English
burlesque. Early in 1929 I communicated this project to Leacock. His answer was contained in a postscript to a formal
letter about copyright.

> *P.S. Don't* publish a history of burlesque as a preface: it's too
> good; if you do it well and AMUSINGLY (to hell with
> *accurately*) it would have a real sale.

So the plays were published separately; and I set off on a
long adventure which has led from the domed reading-room
of the British Museum to the cool vault of the Lord Chamberlain's collection at St. James's Palace.

The vastness of the subject, the writing of other works, the
necessity of earning a living, and the distractions of a war, have
spread those researches over more than twenty years. When I
began no-one (so far as I could find) had ever tackled the
subject of burlesque apart from parody. In the years between,
three books have appeared—*A Survey of Burlesque and Parody in
English* by George Kitchin (1931) ; Richmond P. Bond's *English
Burlesque Poetry 1700–1750* (1932) and *The Novel in Motley* by
Archibald Bolling Shepperson (1936). But two of these books
are not concerned with the theatre, and Dr. Kitchin's survey,
wide as it is, deliberately excludes dramatic burlesque. The
book which Stephen Leacock advised me to write, twenty-two
years ago, has not yet been written by anyone.

I hope that the facts in this book are reliable; but (to hell
with accurately) I have not attempted any painstaking accumu-
lation of dates and publications and first performances. This
is not a history of theatrical events, but a review of critical
laughter, an attempt to trace the pedigree of dramatic burlesque, to mark family features and record favourite traditions.

At one time I considered the construction of similar pedigrees for prose burlesque, but, although *The Novel in Motley* has dealt admirably with a part of this problem, it still remains too large a subject to confine in only half a book. There are pedigrees of heroines and hypocrites, of lawyers, reviewers and colonels, of preachers and pedants and pamphleteers. It would be pleasant, for instance, to trace, by way of Sterne's Slawkenbergius, the distant origins of Dr. Strabismus of Utrecht (whom God preserve); or to compare the views of Dr. Caliban and Mr. Lambkin with those of Martinus Scriblerus and the author of *Advice to a Young Reviewer*, published at Oxford in 1807.

But not now: this book is about burlesque in the theatre after 1660.

In the many quotations included in these pages I have occasionally adjusted the punctuation and the spelling.

THE PICTURES

The five illustrations by George Cruikshank have been reproduced from copies in the British Museum. "The Stage Sailor" and "The Stage Countryman" are from *George Cruikshank's Table Book* (1845) and were illustrations to burlesque sketches by Gilbert A'Beckett. The *Tom Thumb* ghost picture and the *Bombastes Furioso* picture are from Cruikshank's illustrated editions of those plays (1830). The etching of Mrs. Liston as Queen Dollalolla was made for *The British Stage* in 1817.

The picture of Richard Suett as Bayes is an engraving by W. Skelton of a painting by John Graham. It is reproduced from a copy in the Raymond Mander and Joe Mitchenson Collection. The original is in the Victoria and Albert Museum.

The portrait of Miss Rose as Tom Thumb is reproduced from a copy in the Cheylesmore collection at the British Museum. It was painted by John Berridge and engraved by Edward Fisher in 1770. Nothing is known of this infant—except that she played the Duke of York and one other character at the Haymarket in 1769.

The portrait of Charles Mathews as Sir Fretful Plagiary is copied from the picture by Samuel de Wilde at The Garrick Club. This picture stands a little apart from the others, for Sir Fretful is not a character in Puff's play and does not belong to the main burlesque of *The Critic*. But he is an essentially burlesque character and this portrait is an unforgettably good representation of the important basic burlesque joke of pomposity.

The photographs of Sir Ralph Richardson as Burleigh and Sir Laurence Olivier as Puff were taken by Mr. John Vickers during the Old Vic production of *The Critic* in 1945–6.

More must be written of the three remaining pictures, none of which has been reproduced before.

The *Chrononhotonthologos* picture is taken from a design attributed to Henri Gravelot (1699–1773). It was published as a frontispiece to the first edition of the play (1734), but with the addition of a fourth figure on the left of the engraving. Gravelot's original design is reproduced for the first time in this book.

Mr. Leonard Duke, C.B.E., to whom the *Chrononhotonthologos* picture belongs, is also the owner of the water-colour by Rowlandson, "Modern Grace—or the Operatical Finale of the Ballet of Alonzo e cara". The title "Alonzo e cara", with a small 'c', had struck both Mr. Duke and myself as highly peculiar, for it was not a name and it did not make any other kind of sense. It was, therefore, with considerable excitement that I discovered (while looking for something else) that Gillray had published in 1796 a cartoon called "Modern Grace, or the Operatical Finale to the ballet of Alonzo e caro" (with an 'o'). Pursuing this mystery, Mr. Duke then found that the Gillray cartoon was a burlesque of the ballet "Alonzo e Cora", produced by Didelot at the Opera House in 1796, and that the Rowlandson cartoon was an adaptation of the Gillray picture; and the fortunate chance that someone long ago had written the names in a copy of Gillray's works at the British Museum establishes the figures (*l.* to *r.*) as Mlle Rose, Didelot, and Mlle Parisot. The Rowlandson is a softer, merrier picture than that by Gillray, but in putting 'cara' he seems to have failed to see Gillray's joke: 'caro', as distant memories of a classical education enabled Mr. Duke to recall, is Latin for 'flesh'.

The other Rowlandson picture has an equally curious

history. When I first saw it at the Arts' Council exhibition of Mr.
Gilbert Davis's collection in the autumn of 1950 neither the
play nor the theatre were recorded. I recognized that the play
was *Tom Thumb*, the burletta by Kane O'Hara, adapted from
Fielding's original work and first produced at Covent Garden
in 1780. The pile of bodies could only belong to a farce or a
burlesque, and it exactly represents the carnage at the end of
the piece when everyone assassinates somebody. There should
be six bodies, two male and four female—and, though it takes
a little working out with a magnifying glass, six bodies there
certainly are. Before them stands the king, ranting his last lines
and about to stab himself. He wears a full-bottomed wig, and a
full-bottomed wig for King Arthur was one of the traditions of
the play. The feathered head and the large posterior betrays
the queen. Queen Dollalolla always wore feathers—witness the
picture of Mrs. Liston. Finally, the elaborate crown over the
mirror identifies the scene as the Royal Presence Chamber—
which is where it should be.

The play established, it was necessary to identify the theatre,
and my attention was drawn by Mr. Richard Southern to the
curious fact that the drawing is closely similar to a picture
published by Ackermann in 1813 in a book called *Poetical
Sketches of Scarborough, illustrated by twenty-one engravings of Humor-
ous Subjects coloured from original designs made upon the spot by J.
Green and etched by T. Rowlandson.* The engraving of the Scarborough Theatre turns out to be this very subject, *Tom Thumb*
included—indeed the play is specifically named in the verses.

There is some mystery about this publication, for the names
J. Bluck and J. C. Stadler are attached to no less than sixteen
of the etchings. The picture of the theatre is one of the remaining five to which no name other than Green's is attached. If
Rowlandson did etch this rather flat picture by Green he must
subsequently have drawn an adaptation of it for his own amuse-
ment, perhaps because somebody wanted the picture from his
own hand. The design is the same, but where Green has thirty-
six people in the boxes, Rowlandson has fifty-six; all Rowlandson's figures are more strongly characterized than Green's; and
the scene on the stage has a much richer burlesque exaggeration. The comic catastrophe of *Tom Thumb* might be conducted
in many ways, but we now know that the Georgian joke

consisted in piling the bodies up on top of each other, a rubbish heap of legs, backsides and feathers. It is not often that one finds unrebuttable evidence of so fugitive an art as stage comic business.[1]

It has been my object to choose pictures which exactly reflect the title of this book—*The Burlesque Tradition*. Each picture illustrates a principal joke in the burlesque canon, except only the portrait of Miss Rose as Tom Thumb, and that exhibits the extravagant costume traditional for the part.

For permission to reproduce these pictures my thanks are due to the Keeper of the Prints at the British Museum, the Committee of the Garrick Club, Mr. John Vickers, Mr. Raymond Mander and Mr. Joe Mitchenson, Mr. Leonard Duke, C.B.E., and Mr. Gilbert Davis. I am additionally grateful to Mr. Duke and Mr. Davis for many civilities which have greatly assisted me in assembling these pictures.

Finally, for permission to include the quotations from the works of the late Stephen Leacock I am indebted both to his American and his English publishers, Dodd Mead and Company, Inc., New York, and John Lane, the Bodley Head Limited, London.

V. C. CLINTON-BADDELEY

[1] The original picture in the Ackermann publication of 1813 is reproduced in *Theatre Notebook*, Vol. I, No. 5, p. 60, October 1946.

CONTENTS

PART ONE

INTRODUCTORY

PART TWO

THE BURLESQUE TRADITION IN THE ENGLISH THEATRE AFTER 1660

ILLUSTRATIONS

xv

INTRODUCTORY

THE NATURE OF BURLESQUE

THERE is a cleavage in humour between those arts which derive laughter from truth and those which derive it from fancy. Pure comedy is the reflection of nature, but there are sub-divisions of comedy which are nothing of the kind. Epigrammatic comedy endows its characters with unnatural gifts of wit; sentimental comedy idealizes life to create a story more agreeable than the lot of common experience, presenting as truth a picture of possible but improbable behaviour; and farce, recognizing no code of behaviour whatever, presents a picture of life which is neither probable nor possible. In varying degree each is the reflection of an entertaining falsehood.

To these arts satire bears no relationship, for satire has no meaning except as the reflection of truth. The Private Secretary and Charley's Aunt inhabit a mad world irreconcilably divided from ours, but Becky Sharp and Mr. Peachum are marked and familiar members of society. Farce and comedy have no purpose in the world but to amuse. Satire is actuated by a burning desire to rebuke and to reform, " to lash in general the reigning and fashionable vices and recommend and set virtue in as amiable a light as possible".[1]

Like satire, burlesque employs laughter as criticism and reflects truth rather than the artificial or the ideal; but in every other purpose and method the two arts are entirely different. "The chief end I propose to myself in all my labours is to vex the world rather than divert it," wrote Swift.[2] "The stage, sir," wrote Gay,[1] "hath the privilege of the pulpit to attack vice however dignified or distinguished, and preachers and poets should not be too well bred upon these occasions. Nobody can overdo it when he attacks the vice and not the person." Such is satire, violent and angry: but burlesque is never angry, because its criticism is directed not against faults of virtue, but against

---

[1] Preface to *Polly* by John Gay (1729).
[2] Letter to Pope, September 29, 1725.

I

faults of style and of humour. It wants to destroy nothing—not even sententiousness, its dearest enemy: for if sententiousness were dead there would be one less joke in the world to laugh at. Burlesque serves truth, not with the bitterness of its tongue, but with the irreverence and deliberate impropriety of its laughter. Satire is the schoolmaster attacking dishonesty with a whip. Burlesque is the rude boy attacking pomposity with a pea-shooter. Satire holds up the multiple mirror of the tailor's shop, pitilessly revealing shameful idiosyncrasies. Burlesque holds up the concave mirror and shows the world, not how contemptible it is, but how funny. Satire must laugh not to weep.[1] Burlesque must laugh not to burst—and best of all it likes to laugh among friends, for burlesque discovers laughter not in the objects of its hatred but rather in the objects of its affection: and that is the abiding difference between the two arts.

Unfortunately this distinction is frequently obliterated in criticism by an interchangeable use of the adjectives "burlesque" and "satirical". The misconception is a common one —but when Shakespeare's *Troilus and Cressida* is classed as a burlesque of Homer[2] it is time to define the word more closely. Critics have argued about this bitter and lovely play for centuries. Some have supposed it a satire of Troy, some a satire of Shakespeare's own contemporaries, some a satire of war: but —except where Thersites imitates the beef-witted Ajax—no-one could truly discover a glint of the good humour of burlesque.[3]

> Time hath, my Lord, a wallet at his back,
> Wherein he puts alms for oblivion,
> A great-siz'd monster of ingratitudes:
> Those scraps are good deeds past; which are devour'd
> As fast as they are made, forgot as soon
> As done: perseverance, dear my Lord,
> Keeps honour bright: to have done, is to hang
> Quite out of fashion, like a rusty mail
> In monumental mockery.

---

[1] And if I laugh at any mortal thing
'Tis that I may not weep.
(BYRON: *Don Juan*, c4, v4.)

[2] *Pons Assinorum or the Future of Nonsense* by G. Edinger & E. J. C. Neep (1929).

[3] Some critics believe Ajax to be a burlesque portrait of Ben Jonson.

Is this a burlesque of wisdom? Or this a burlesque of love?

> Injurious time now with a robber's haste
> Crams his rich thievery up, he knows not how:
> As many farewells as be stars in heaven,
> With distinct breath and consign'd kisses to them,
> He fumbles up into a loose adieu,
> And scants us with a single famish'd kiss
> Distasted with the salt of broken tears.

Dickens satirized the Yorkshire schools in Dotheboys Hall.

"We'll put you into your regular bedroom tomorrow, Nickleby," said Squeers. "Let me see! who sleeps in Brooks's bed, my dear?"

"Brooks's," said Mrs. Squeers pondering. "There's Jennings, little Bolder, Graymarsh, and what's his name."

"So there is," rejoined Squeers. "Yes! Brooks is full. . . . There's a place somewhere, I know . . . but I can't at the moment call to mind where it is. However, we'll have all that settled tomorrow. Goodnight, Nickleby. Seven o'clock in the morning mind . . . I'll come in myself, and show you where the well is. . . . You'll always find a bit of soap in the kitchen window. . . . I don't know, I am sure, whose towel to put you on; but if you'll make shift with something tomorrow morning, Mrs. Squeers will arrange that in the course of the day. My dear, don't forget."

"I'll take care," replied Mrs. Squeers; "and mind you take care, young man, and get first wash. The teacher ought always to have it; but they get the better of him if they can."

We laugh at that. But we "laugh not to weep"—not to stamp and shout with fury, because we know that, in spite of an air of comicality, the picture is true and not a monstrous invention of Dickens, as many smug and comfortable people have supposed. In the Yorkshire schools a hundred and thirty years ago the boys did lie five in a bed, and did have only two towels between the lot of them, and did suffer as fiercely as did the boys at "Dotheboys Hall, in the delightful village of Dotheboys, near Greta Bridge in Yorkshire". During the publication of *Nickleby*, Charles Dickens wrote to a friend "Depend upon it that the rascalities of these Yorkshire schoolmasters *cannot* easily be exaggerated, and that I have kept down the strong truth and thrown as much comicality over it as I could." [1] As much as he could: he was not out to laugh.

[1] Charles Dickens to Mrs. Hall, December 29, 1838.

The fact is that the arrangements discussed by Mr. and Mrs. Squeers, on the night of the arrival of Nicholas Nickleby at Dotheboys Hall, are exactly paralleled by the evidence of child witnesses in the newspaper reports of *Jones v. Shaw* and *Ockerly v. Shaw*, two suits against a Yorkshire schoolmaster, heard in the Court of Common Pleas on October 30 and 31, 1823. Even the famous advertisement for Mr. Wackford Squeers' Academy is closely modelled on advertisements inserted in *The Times* by this same Shaw and others like him, all doing a roaring business on the principle of low fees and no vacations.

Satire is brimstone, but burlesque is wine. It was in an entirely different spirit that Dickens laughed about the Crummles theatrical company. He loved the theatre, and he laughed at its absurdities not because he wanted to destroy them but because he knew that they were funny. Take Mr. Folair's confident request for a dance in the middle of a serious drama.

"I must have a dance of some kind, you know," said Mr. Folair. "You'll have to introduce one for the phenomenon, so you'd better make a *pas de deux*, and save time."

"There's nothing easier than that," said Mr. Lenville, observing the disturbed looks of the young dramatist.

"Upon my word I don't see how it's to be done," rejoined Nicholas.

"Why isn't it obvious?" reasoned Mr. Lenville. "Gadzooks, who can help seeing the way to do it?—you astonish me! You get the distressed lady, and the little child, and the attached servant, into the poor lodgings, don't you?—Well, look here. The distressed lady sinks into a chair and buries her face in her pocket handkerchief— 'What makes you weep, mama?' says the child. 'Don't weep, mama, or you'll make me weep too!'—'And me!' says the faithful servant, rubbing his eyes with his arm. 'What can we do to raise your spirits, dear mama?' says the little child. 'Aye, what *can* we do?' says the faithful servant. 'Oh, Pierre,' says the distressed lady; 'would that I could shake off these painful thoughts!'—'Try, ma'am, try,' says the faithful servant; 'rouse yourself, ma'am; be amused.' 'I will,' says the lady, 'I will learn to suffer with fortitude. Do you remember that dance, my honest friend, which, in happier days, you practised with this sweet angel? It never failed to calm my spirits then. Oh! let me see it once again before I die!' There it is—cue for the band, *before I die*—and off they go. That's the regular thing; isn't it Tommy?"

"That's it," replied Mr. Folair. "The distressed lady, overpowered by old recollections, faints at the end of the dance, and you close in with a picture."

The exact art of burlesque is not easy to define clearly, because at different times the word has been used to mean different things. The name is derived from the Italian *burlesco* from *burla*, a joke; but because men follow various fashions in what they think funny, burlesque has been variously interpreted in different centuries. In the 17th century the word was at first taken to mean the debasement of classical writers, as in the many travesties of Vergil. In the 18th century it included also the reverse of the travesty, the mock-heroic, in which the grand manner is expended upon a mean subject, as in *The Rape of the Lock*. In the 20th century these original manifestations of burlesque are almost unknown. In this age, though occasionally found to great advantage in the novel, burlesque has been chiefly located in the theatre.

Fielding defines burlesque as "what is monstrous and unnatural, and where our delight, if we examine it, arises from the surprising absurdity, as in appropriating the manners of the highest to the lowest, or *e converso*". He then compares it with 'caricatura' whose aim he says "is to exhibit monsters, not men; and all distortions and exaggerations whatever are within its province".[1]

That definition may have been sufficient for the more malicious practice of the 18th century. Today it is certainly incomplete, because, while emphasizing the distortion of burlesque and caricature, it omits to recognize the sincerity which is essential to the practice of both arts. Caricature and burlesque exhibit "all distortions and exaggerations whatever", but under this discipline—that they purpose that way to get closer to essential truth. Caricature and burlesque set out to excite laughter by the subtle distortion of salient characteristics—but that laughter is not obtained by the exhibition of "the monstrous and the unnatural". On the contrary it springs from the essential closeness of the joke to the original. Low's Colonel Blimp is funny because he is familiar. A man in woman's clothes is funny because of his likeness to the feminine, not because of his unlikeness. A woman in the part of Widow Twankey is never convincing, because she obscures her femininity in the act of making herself grotesque. Mr. Lenville's recipe for introducing the *pas de deux* into a serious drama is a burlesque of theatrical

[1] Preface to *Joseph Andrews*.

convention a hundred years ago. The joke rests upon the fact
that the description is pleasantly near the truth.

Scenic effects and transformations were dear to Dickens.
The good ones excited him. The bad ones made him laugh.
"You couldn't sing a comic song on the pony's back could
you?" said Mr. Crummles as he considered suggestions for
Nicholas Nickleby's farewell performance.

"No," replied Nicholas, "I couldn't indeed."

"It has drawn money before now," said Mr. Crummles, with a
look of disappointment. "What do you think of a brilliant display
of fireworks? . . . Eighteen pence would do it. . . . You on the top
of a pair of steps with the phenomenon in an attitude; 'Farewell' on
a transparency behind; and nine people at the wings with a squib
in each hand—all the dozen and a half going off at once—it would
be very grand—awful from the front, quite awful."

Dickens plainly liked Mr. Crummles. Pope, the satirist, was
impelled by entirely different emotions when he wrote about
Rich, the harlequin.

> Yet would'st thou more? In yonder cloud behold,
> Whose sars'net skirts are edg'd with flamy gold,
> A matchless youth! his nod these worlds controls,
> Wings the red lightning, and the thunder rolls.
> Angel of Dulness, sent to scatter round
> Her magic charms o'er all unclassic ground:
> Yon stars, yon suns, he rears at pleasure higher,
> Illumes their light, and sets their flames on fire.
> Immortal Rich! how calm he sits at ease
> 'Mid snows of paper, and fierce hail of pease;
> And proud his Mistress' orders to perform,
> Rides in the whirlwind, and directs the storm.[1]

A smaller distinction must be made between burlesque and
parody. Satire and burlesque are distant relations. Parody and
burlesque are mother and child. But burlesque has acquired a
different habit of laughter. Parody criticises the letter of a work
of art; burlesque criticises the spirit. Traditional stories with no
familiar original—such as *The Babes in the Wood*—cannot be

---

[1] The Italian opera and pantomime are attacked in *The Dunciad*, Bk. 3,
233–316, and Bk. 4, 45–70.

parodied at all. But they can be burlesqued, and have been for pantomime purposes again and again.

Parody, the oldest and most obvious form of irreverence, is short, direct and particular. It fastens itself upon an exact subject and guys it line by line, as Calverley did in his magnificent imitation of Browning's *The Ring and the Book*.

> You see this pebble-stone? It's a thing I bought
> Of a bit of a chit of a boy i' the mid o' the day—
> I like to dock the smaller parts-o'-speech,
> As we curtail the already cur-tail'd cur
> (You catch the paronomasia, play 'po' words?)
> Did, rather, i' the pre-Landseerian days.
> Well, to my muttons.   I purchased the concern,
> And clapt it i' my poke, having given for same,
> By way o' chop, swop, barter or exchange—
> "Chop" was my snickering dandiprat's own term—
> One shilling and fourpence, current coin o' the realm.
> O—n—e one and f—o—u—r four
> Pence, one and fourpence—you are with me, Sir?
> What hour it skills not: ten or eleven o' the clock,
> One day (and what a roaring day it was
> Go shop or sight-see—bar a spit o' rain!)
> In February, eighteen sixty nine,
> Alexandrina Victoria, Fidei
> Hm—hm—how runs the jargon? being on the throne.

In the 129 lines of *The Cock and the Bull* 104 references have been traced to passages in *The Ring and the Book*, collected throughout the whole length of that 21,000 line poem.[1] The last two lines of the quotation, for instance, are a reflection of

> Francesca Camilla Vittoria Angela
> Pompilia Comparini,—laughable!

Burlesque is something different from this. It is wider in its range, aims to reduce a vast subject to essentials and laughs at once at a whole theory of writing. The spirit of a hundred folk songs is exposed in one mock lyric. Heroic tragedy as a whole art is travestied in the rhymed couplets of extravaganza. "Beachcomber" in one paragraph betrays the whole tribe of

[1] See *Browning and Calverley or Poem and Parody* by Percy L. Babington (1925).

paragraph writers. Stephen Leacock in a single sketch discovers the fundamental weakness of all detective stories. Max Beerbohm reflects whole periods of literature in the poetry of Enoch Soames and Savonarola Brown. Jane Austen explodes the romantic novel in a single sentence: "The noble Youth informed us that his name was Lindsay—for particular reasons however I shall conceal it under that of Talbot." [1]

Burlesque is laughter for laughter's sake: and it is not often antagonistic. John Philips could never have written *The Splendid Shilling* (1701) if he had not been a great admirer of Milton.

> My galligaskins, that have long withstood
> The winter's fury and encroaching frosts,
> By time subdued (what will not time subdue!)
> An horrid chasm disclose, with orifice,
> Wide, discontinuous; at which the winds
> Eurus and Auster, and the dreadful force
> Of Boreas, that congeals the Cronian waves,
> Tumultuous enter, with dire chilling blasts
> Portending agues. Thus a well-fraught ship
> Long sailed secure, or through th' Aegean deep
> Or the Ionian . . .

And so the imagery piles up to build a tremendous parallel with a hole in a gentleman's trousers.

Nor is there anything offensive about S. Bagot de la Bere's analysis of Hilaire Belloc.

. . . But for my part I set my face to the sun and my back to the south wind, and, walking swiftly, came that evening to my home in the Good Country (for so we call Sussex—or at least that part of it where I live, at Piddinghoe, below Arundel).

And when I had drunk some ale I went to bed.

But before I slept I composed a lament for the souls of those who are not of Sussex, but live and die *in partibus infidelium*, particularly the men of Kent, who (as is commonly reported) fry pig's feet with butter and have their wives in common.

So, commending myself to the saints and singing very joyfully, I fell asleep.

True burlesque is written with love; direct parody is often laughter with a sting in it. Henry Carey felt no secondary

---

[1] *Love and Freindship.*

feeling of admiration for his subject when he parodied Ambrose
Phillips, and added 'Namby-Pamby' to the English language.

> All ye Poets of the Age!
> All ye Witlings of the Stage!
> Learn your jingles to reform!
> Crop your numbers and Conform!
> Let your little Verses flow
> Gently, Sweetly, Row by Row:
> Let the verse the Subject fit;
> Little Subject, Little Wit.[1]

'Namby-Pamby' (supposed to be a baby's articulation of the
name Ambrose Phillips) was a parody of a group of sycophantic
verses written in little words and little lines, addressed to Miss
Carteret, youthful daughter of a conveniently influential father.
The whole poem is critical and devastatingly offensive.

At the other end of the century the admirable poetry of the
Anti-Jacobin[2] was a scourge not only for the Opposition but
for the English poets. *The Loves of the Triangles* ridicules Erasmus
Darwin's *The Loves of the Plants. The Progress of Man* parodies
Payne Knight's *Progress of Civil Society. The Friend of Humanity
and the Needy Knife Grinder* was a simultaneous slap at the Rights
of Man and at Robert Southey's entirely unsuitable English
Sapphics.[3]

> "Needy Knife-grinder! whither are you going?
> Rough is the road, your wheel is out of order—
> Bleak blows the blast: your hat has got a hole in 't,
> So have your breeches!" . . .

J. K. Stephens' Wordsworthian sonnet, "Two voices are
there", and H. Duff Traill's ballad "after Dilettante Concetti",

---

[1] Printed 1729.
[2] Published between November 1797 and July 1798.
[3]   Cold was the night wind; drifting fast the snows fell;
        Wide were the downs, and shelterless and naked;
        When a poor wand'rer struggled on her journey,
            Weary and way-sore.

        Drear were the downs, more dreary her reflections;
        Cold was the night wind, colder was her bosom:
        She had no home, the world was all before her,
            She had no shelter.
                    etc.

are equally pickled in vinegar. Stephens contrasted the mighty voice of Wordsworth with that other voice "of an old half-witted sheep" complacently baa-ing banalities. Traill attacked the bogus ballad. An essential part of certain ancient ballads is their repetitions and refrains. They were meant to be sung and there was nothing ridiculous about them. The creation of refrains which were meant only to be read Traill considered an ignorant affectation, and his reply to *Sister Helen* had no undercurrent of admiration in it.

> "Why do you wear your hair like a man,
>   Sister Helen?
> This week is the third since you began."
> "I'm writing a ballad: be still if you can
>   Little brother.
>   (*O Mother Carey, mother!*
> *What chickens are these between sea and heaven?*)"
>
> "But why does your figure appear so lean,
>   Sister Helen?
> And why do you dress in sage, sage green?"
> "Children should never be heard, if seen,
>   Little brother.
>   (*O Mother Carey, Mother!*
> *What fowls are abroad in the stormy heaven!*)"

A deficiency in humour is a deficiency in perception, an admitted calamity, which accounts for the fact that people who would never claim to be clever or generous or unselfish are always ready to declare a "keen sense of humour". Actors, in particular, cherish a belief in their own exceptional gift for burlesque. In fact there is no rarer talent in the whole equipment of the actor, for the technique of burlesque is an exact technique, a regular knife-edge of good judgement. Under-played, or under-written—the effect is the same in both departments of the art—burlesque means nothing. Over-played, or over-written, it becomes that catastrophic thing, a joke explained.

The best burlesque supports an elaborate pretence of not being funny at all, and leaves audience or reader in a happy state of uncertainty whether good sense has been outraged or not.

In a Cambridge burlesque of *Oedipus Tyrannus* the inevitable altar in the centre of the stage bore the legend "Commit no Nemesis", an entirely reasonable request. And it is difficult to criticize the logic of Edwards, the baffled police officer, in Leacock's burlesque murder mystery *Who d'you think did it?*

"The window has apparently been opened from the outside, sir, the sash being lifted with a knife or other sharp instrument. The dust on the sill outside has been disturbed as if by a man of extra-ordinary agility lying on his stomach—don't bother about that Mr. Kent—it's *always there.*"

"True; so it is . . . Ha! did you see that trap-door?"

"We did. The dust around the rim has been disturbed. The trap opens into a hollow in the roof. A man of extraordinary dexterity might open the trap with a billiard-cue, throw up a fine manilla rope, climb up the rope and lie there on his stomach—for the matter of that, look at this huge old-fashioned fireplace; a man of extraordinary precocity could climb up the chimney—or this dumb waiter for serving drinks, leading down to the maid's quarters; a man of extraordinary indelicacy might ride up and down on it."

The shadow of a grin upon the face of innocence is main-tained in the same way in Stella Gibbons' *Cold Comfort Farm*, with its nearly right pastoral language—agricultural instru-ments, like 'scranlet' and 'rennet-post'; birds and flowers like 'marsh-tigget', 'dogs-fennel', and 'beard's-crow'; diseases like 'Queen's Bane', and 'Prince's Forfeit'—words that lodge a legitimate criticism but at the same time lend a bucolic and botanical authenticity to the whole imposture.

Monseigneur Knox, in his *Essays in Satire*, has argued that humour, apart from satire, belongs to the English-speaking peo-ples alone. It is at least certain that burlesque is a joke which can flourish only in a free and prosperous democracy, and that, in the absence of free democracies among the governments of the world, it has become a joke peculiarly British. The prime objects of its raillery are sententiousness and pomposity, faults of humour much found among the holders of high authority; and since burlesque is no respecter of persons, it naturally follows that a country which enjoys licensed impudence can afford to do so. Those in authority, who are not at all sure how long they will stay there, are not so tolerant of even friendly criticism—which is the explanation of the fact that the stage humour of many countries is limited to witty comedy, and the safe inanities of farce. It is not that the totalitarian state is an unsuitable subject for the burlesque artist, but that the burlesque artist is an unsuitable subject for the totalitarian state.

Herr Werner Finck, the German actor, discovered this fact in 1935 when his cabaret was closed and he himself imprisoned in Dachau for attempting to "make party and State institutions ridiculous". As Dr. Goebbels said, "There were certain values in the life of a nation which must remain untouched by cynics."[1] Cleon had made a similar pronouncement in 426 B.C. after the production of *The Babylonians*, as Aristophanes subsequently declared in *The Acharnians*.[2]

> Aye and I know what I myself endured
> At Cleon's hands for last year's comedy.
> How to the Council house he haled me off,
> And slanged, and lied, and slandered, and
>   betongued me.

And again,

> Bear me no grudge, spectators, if, a beggar,
> I dare to speak before the Athenian people
> About the city in a comic play.
> For what is true even comedy can tell.
> And I shall utter startling things but true.
> Nor now can Cleon slander me because,
> With strangers present, I defame the State.

Aristophanes remained to laugh in Athens for many years, but the unhappy Finck was in the news again in 1939, when it was announced that he had been excluded from the Reich Chamber of Culture.

It is now officially stated that he has "failed despite this warning, to reveal a positive attitude towards National Socialism, and has caused great public offence, particularly among members of the party".

Dr. Goebbels' action has caused some surprise in Berlin stage circles. During the past year or two greater latitude has been permitted in making mild fun of certain aspects of the Nazi system.

[1] November 23rd, 1938.
[2] *The Acharnians*, lines 377–80, and 596–602. The quotations are from the translation by Benjamin Bickley Rogers.

It was beginning to be thought that, after six years in power, the regime was now strong enough to allow this form of criticism as a safety-valve.

In an article which will appear tomorrow in the *Voelkischer Beobachter* under the heading "Have we still got a sense of humour?" Dr. Goebbels says questions like the colonial problem or the four years' plan are too serious to be the subject of would-be funny chatter in a smoky cabaret.

He threatens to take action against the audiences which like to listen to such jokes, and which, he says, consist almost entirely of the one per cent of the nation that still votes "No." in plebiscites and Reichstag elections.[1]

"I believe the glory of sporting with sacred things is peculiar to the English nation!" wrote John Wesley in his diary on June 26, 1738. The same view has often been held by bewildered Europeans. In the war of 1914 the Germans were unable to understand how the British soldier could sing The Hymn of Hate with its terrible refrain, "Gott straffe England". True to type, in 1940 they produced another word intended to freeze the marrow and to tighten the breath. It suffered the same fate. Blitzkreig was immediately accepted with gratitude as a new ornament for the English tongue.

The European is confounded by this British flippancy. He fails to understand how a nation of such imperial proportions can poke fun at retired colonels and patriotic songs, and permit the appearance of Britannia as a comic figure on the stage. He does not perceive that the British laugh about important things to save them from the canker of sentimentality. They laugh at things they like in order to keep them as they like them. The portentous Imperialist is mocked that the Empire may survive even the injury of his drivelling enthusiasms, and Britannia becomes a figure of fun because she can afford to be generous about it. There would be nothing funny about a Britannia in defeat.

Burlesque has a licence in Britain to laugh obliquely at sacred things—not laughing in reality at the things themselves, but at those enthusiasts who make a noble thing undignified by the warmth of their admiration. There was nothing wrong with the rhymed heroic couplet as used in epic or didactic poetry. There

---

[1] *Daily Telegraph.* February 4th, 1939.

was all the world wrong with it when a form of expression
peculiarly suited to wit and antithesis was used by dunces as a
vehicle for portentous tragedy. It is not the measure but the
monstrous use of it which burlesque exposes in the rhymed
couplets of old extravaganza. Nor does burlesque deny the
decent virtues of masculine honour and feminine modesty.
What it exposes is the false sentiment about these virtues which
abounded in old melodramas. There was nothing wrong with
folk-songs and folk-dances until their performers began to treat
a diversion as a religious exercise. Nor was there anything
wrong with the charming legends of our island fairies until a
lot of old women made them ridiculous by falsely pretending
to believe in them. So, one by one, do honourable subjects
become a matter for laughter.

THE PROGRESS OF BURLESQUE

THE history of burlesque is long—but it is not so long as the
history of intellectual pride, sententiousness, pomposity, and all
the other false dignities which are its natural prey. For burlesque flourishes in the warm atmosphere of tolerance, and
tolerance is a luxury derived from security after generations of
private discipline. There is no humour in the stark legends of
ancient peoples. There is no humour in Homer; but at the
height of Greek civilization the plays of Aristophanes contained
every known element of laughter. The themes were satirical;
there was farce and comedy in their unfolding, and parody in
their language.   Burlesque was introduced as a separate joke
in certain typical character studies: the miniature part of
Nicarcus [1] in *The Acharnians*, and the bunch of absurdities in
The Birds, the priest, the poet, Meton the astronomer,[1] the
commissioner, Cinesias, and the sycophant; in certain technical jokes such as the speech of the sausage-seller in *The
Knights*,[2] a plain burlesque of the speech of a tragic messenger;
and in the lyrics sung by Aeschylus and Euripides in *The Frogs*.[3]

[1] See pp. 19–20 for a comparison with *Volpone* and *Everyman out of his humour*.
[2] Lines 624–682.
[3] *The Acharnians* 425 B.C., *The Knights* 424 B.C., *The Birds* 414 B.C., *The
Frogs* 405 B.C.

But the decay of the Greek drama went swiftly in time with the decay of the Greek state. Satire was killed by censorship. Burlesque yielded to mild comedy and mild comedy gave place to a farce which contained no flavour of critical tannin. It was this drama which the Latin authors translated for the Roman audience, whose principal entertainment consisted in spectacle, combat, buffoonery, pantomime and farce. Satire and burlesque were dangerous amusements in a city where an incautious playwright could be burnt alive at the order of a crazy dictator.

The ancient theatre was destroyed by the ignorance and neglect of the Barbarian invaders, and by the hostility of the Christian Church. Such traditions as survived for the entertainment of the Dark Ages were preserved by acrobats, contortionists, tumblers, jugglers, ballad-singers and bear-leaders. There was nothing of the art of burlesque in them. Nor were the medieval revels of the Feast of Fools and the Boy Bishop much nearer to critical laughter. The key phrase of the Feast of Fools, "Deposuit," "He hath put down the mighty from their seat," is certainly a perfect motto for burlesque. But the niceties of laughter were as yet undeveloped. Priests and clerks in masks or dressed as women—playing at dice at the altar—censing "with stinking smoke from the soles of old shoes"—driving through the town, raising laughter "in infamous performances with indecent gestures and scurrilous and unchaste words": [1] all this may have been vastly entertaining, but the humour of it was one-quarter crude parody and three-quarters horseplay. There was sometimes laughter of a better sort in the plays of saints and bible stories which formed the material of the miracle plays and pageants, but though the Widow Twankey might trace a long ancestry back to Mrs. Noah who appears in *Noah's Flood*, true burlesque is nowhere characteristic either of the miracle plays or of the interludes which followed them. Heywood's "mery playe betwene the pardoner and the frere the curate and neybour PRATTE" [2] is plain knock-about farce.

PARSON: Help! help! Neighbour Pratte! Neighbour Pratte!
              In the worship of God, help me somewhat!

---

[1] Letter of the Faculty of Theology in the University of Paris addressed to the Bishops, March 12, 1445.   [2] Published 1533.

PRATTE: Nay, deal as thou cans't with that elf,
           For why I have enough to do myself!
           Alas! for pain I am almost dead,
           The red blood so runneth down about my head,
           Nay, and thou cans't, I pray thee, help me!

PARSON: Nay, by the mass, fellow, it will not be!
           I have more tow on my distaff than I can well spin!
           The cursed friar doth the upper hand win!

FRIAR: Will ye leave then, and let us in peace depart?

PARSON &
PRATTE: Yes, by our Lady, even with all our heart!

FRIAR &
PARDONER: Then, adieu, to the devil, till he come again.

PARSON &
PRATTE: And a mischief go with you both twain.

This is nursery humour. Burlesque is an adult entertainment. Farce raises a laugh from a broken head. Burlesque requires liberty to criticize: the head must be worth breaking.

> Sir Thopas was a doghty swayn,
> Whyt was his face as payndemayn,
>   His lippes rede as rose;
> His rode is lyk scarlet in grayn,
> And I yow telle in good certayn,
>   He hadde a semely nose.

Chaucer's skit on the romances of chivalry is the earliest example of true English burlesque. But Chaucer had no rivals and no immediate successors in this kind of humour. It was impossible that burlesque should flourish widely before the rediscovery of learning and the emancipation of the theatre.

The moment burlesque finds its way on to the English stage, facetiousness makes way for criticism. *The Knight of the Burning Pestle* is a plain burlesque of chivalry and simple people. *Love's Labour's Lost* is a glittering burlesque of fashionable manners, and the entertainment of "The Nine Worthies" is a broad skit of the contemporary pageant.

COSTARD: I Pompey am, Pompey surnam'd the big.
DUMAIN: The great.

COSTARD: It is great, sir; Pompey surnam'd the great;
        That oft in field, with targe and shield, did make my foe
          to sweat;
        And travelling along this coast, I here am come by chance,
        And lay my arms before the legs of this sweet lass of
          France.
        If your ladyship would say "Thanks Pompey", I had done.
PRINCESS: Great thanks, great Pompey.
COSTARD: 'Tis not so much worth; but I hope I was perfect: I made
        a little fault in "great".

All this is criticism: so also is the "Tedious brief scene of young Pyramus and his love Thisbe" in *A Midsummer Night's Dream*, which very tragical mirth is a burlesque on the alliterative and solemn style of such early dramas as *Damon and Pythias*,[1] a play described by its author, Richard Edwards, as "a tragical comedy", and containing in one of its songs a remarkable assembly of the things which Shakespeare thought funny.

> Awake, ye woful wights,
>   That long have wept in woe:
> Resign to me your plaints and tears,
>   My hapless hap to show.
> My woe no tongue can tell,
>   No pen can well descry:
> O, what a death is this to hear,
> Damon my friend must die!
>
> .   .   .   .
>
> Gripe me, you greedy grief
>   And present pangs of death,
> You sisters three, with cruel hands
>   With speed now stop my breath:
> Shrine me in clay alive,
>   Some good man stop mine eye:
> O death, come now, seeing I hear
> Damon my friend must die!

Malone drew attention to certain links between this song and *Pyramus and Thisbe*, but neither he nor Dover Wilson has pointed in particular to the penultimate line. This must be read aloud to be properly savoured. Seeing I hear? Surely these very words were deliberately burlesqued by Shakespeare?

[1] Performed by the Children of the Royal Chapels, probably in 1565.

> I see a voice: now will I to the chink
> To spy an I can hear my Thisbe's face.

Not much early 17th century burlesque is as pleasant or as plain as Shakespeare's.   Too obscure to be understood now, or too savage to be enjoyed, the public bickerings of Marston, Dekker and Jonson, in such plays as *Histriomastix*, *Everyman out of His Humour*, *Poetaster*, *Satiromastix*, with their incidental assaults upon the mannerisms of Gabriel Harvey, the alleged plagiarisms of Samuel Daniel, and the dullness of Anthony Monday, indulge an atrabilious laughter quite wide of burlesque. "My language", writes Jonson in the opening scene of *Everyman out of His Humour*,

> Was never ground into such oyly colours,
> To flatter vice and daube iniquitie:
> But (with an armed and resolved hand)
> Ile strip the ragged follies of the time
> Naked, as at their birth . . . and with a whip of steele
> Print wounding lashes in their yron ribs.

That was Jonson's usual temper, but in certain comedies he drops the fleers and the gibes and the personalities, and decorates his work with genuine burlesque. A palpable ancestor of Dickens's Stiggins is that "notable hypocriticall vermine . . . a fellow of a most arrogant and invincible dulnesse", Zeal-of-the-Land Busy, who comes courting Dame Purecraft in *Bartholomew Fair*. Dame Purecraft's daughter, wishful to go to the Fair, has counterfeited "a woman's longing" to eat pig there. Asked his opinion by the anxious Dame, Zeal-of-the-Land replies:

> Veryily, for the disease of longing, it is a disease, a carnall disease, or appetite, incident to women: and as it is carnall, and incident, it is naturall, very naturall: Now Pigge, it is a meat, and a meat that is nourishing, and may be long'd for, and so consequently eaten: but in the *Fayre*, and as a *Bartholomew*-pig it cannot be eaten, for the very calling it a *Bartholomew*-pigge, and to eat it so, is a spice of *Idolatry*, and you make the *Fayre* no better then one of the high *Places*. This I take it, is the state of the question. A high place.

Later Zeal-of-the-Land conveniently adjusts his opinion, and even accompanies the family thither. "It were a sinne of obstinancy", says the good man, snuffing the air, great obstinancy, high and horrible obstinancy, to decline or resist the titillation of the famelick sense, which is the smell. Therefore be bold (huh, huh, huh) follow the sent. Enter the Tents of the uncleane, for once, and satisfie your wives frailty. Let your fraile wife be satisfied: your zealous mother, and my suffering selfe, will also be satisfied.

Jonson had a particular gift for caricaturing the foolish. In his portrait of Sir Politic Would-be in *Volpone* (lamentably omitted in the most recent revival of the play) he reached out his hand to caress burlesque's favourite child, nit-witted pomposity.

SIR POLITIC: My first is
        Concerning tinder-boxes. You must know
        No family is here without its box.
        Now sir, it being so portable a thing,
        Put case that you or I were ill affected
        Unto the State: Sir, with it in our pockets,
        Might not I go into the Arsenale?
        Or you? Come out again? and none the wiser?
PEREGRINE: Except yourself, sir.
SIR POLITIC: Go to, then. I therefore
        Advertise to the state, how fit it were
        That none but such as were known patriots,
        Sound lovers of their country, should be suffered
        T'enjoy them in their houses; and even those
        Sealed at some office, and at such a bigness
        As might not lurk in pockets.

Solemnity of exactly the same sort had been burlesqued by Aristophanes in the small part of Nicarchus in *The Acharnians*.

NICARCHUS: . . . That lantern-wick will fire the docks.
DICAEOPOLIS: A lantern-wick the docks! O dear, and how?
NICARCHUS: If a Boeotian stuck it in a beetle,
        And sent it, lighted, down a water-course
        Straight to the docks, watching when Boreas blew
        His stiffest breeze, then if the ships caught fire
        They'd blaze up in an instant.[1]

The astronomer Meton, too, in *The Birds* with his

                        So then, observe,
        Applying here my flexible rod, and fixing
        My compass there,—you understand?[1]

---

[1] Translation by Benjamin Bickley Rogers.

is in the style of Sir Politic, explaining his preposterous plan
for avoiding the quarantine at Venice.

> First, I bring in your ship 'twixt two brick walls—
> But these the State shall venture. On the one
> I stretch me a fair tarpaulin, and in that
> I stick my onions, cut in halves; the other
> Is full of loopholes, out of which I thrust
> The noses of my bellows, and those bellows
> I keep, with waterworks, in perpetual motion.

Meton's talk of squaring the circle is also paralleled by Jonson
in his burlesque of academic jargon in *Everyman out of his
Humour.*

Now, sir, whereas the ingenuity of the time and the soul's syn-
derises are but embrions in nature, added to the panch of Esquiline,
and the intervallum of the Zodiac, besides the ecliptic line being
optic, and not mental, but by the contemplative and Theoric part
thereof, doth demonstrate to us the vegetable circumference, and
the ventosity of the tropics, and whereas our intellectual or mincing
capreal (according to the metaphysicks) as you may have read in
Plato's Histriomastix—you conceive me, sir? . . .

The Doctor of Bologna in the Italian commedia dell'arte was
accustomed to talk in precisely this manner. So, later, did the
mock doctor of Molière talk—on the stage of Drury Lane in
1732 in Henry Fielding's adaptation. So, in the 19th century, did
Mr. Cranium talk in *Headlong Hall.* And so, in the 20th century,
do comedians talk on the radio and in the music halls. It is one
of the longest lived jokes in the world.

TRAVESTY AND MOCK-HEROIC

BURLESQUE, then, in its simpler forms, was well known on
the English stage at the beginning of the 17th century: but not
by that name. At that date the word 'burlesque' was unknown
in English, and had only been used experimentally in French.
Pellison-Fontanier, in his *Histoire de l'Académie Française* (1653),
writing of the year 1637, says "ce mot de *Burlesque*, qui étoit
depuis long-temps en Italie, n'avoit pas encore passé les monts".
And Ménage, in *Les Origines de la Langue Françoise* (1660),

writes, "Il n'y a pas long-temps que ce mot *burlesque* est en usage parmy nous: & c'est M. Sarasin qui le premier s'en est servy. Mais c'est M. Scarron qui le premier a pratiqué avec reputation ce genre d'escrire." Correcting these contemporary authorities, Paul Morillot in his *Scarron et le Genre Burlesque* (1888) points to an earlier date and fixes the first use of the word on a different party. It was first written, he says, either "par le vieux d'Aubigné ou par les auteurs de la Satire Menippée."

The first appearance of a word in any language must always remain open to question, but it can at least be gathered from these authorities that the word had been used in French as early as 1594 (the date of the *Satire Menippée*) and that as late as 1637 it was still almost unknown.

It is easier to distinguish the practice of French burlesque. No one disputes that the first French writer to popularize burlesque as a literary form was Scarron, and that the true style is first seen in his *Typhon* published in 1644. The burlesque of Chaucer and Cervantes had smiled at a moribund chivalry. The new burlesque turned its heart to mock at Gods and Heroes. It was a joke which had been popular in Italy for a hundred years before Lalli published his *Eneide Travestita* in 1633. Scarron (who visited Rome in 1635 and must have known this work) produced his *Virgile Travesti* between 1648 and 1652.

The main idea of this vast work is that old joke of the Feast of Fools—Deposuit—He hath put down the mighty from their seat. The *Virgile Travesti* is the *Aeneid* debased and debunked.

> Iris vint au commandement
> De la Dame du Firmament,
> Ou Didon toute agonisante,
> Sur son triste grabat gissante,
> Languissoit fort cruellement,
> Expirant je ne sai comment:
> Elle trouva la pauvre Dame,
> Dont le corps luttant avec l'ame
> Avec d'incroyables efforts
> Souffroit á la fois mille morts.
> Lors elle dit: Je te délivre
> De tout ce qui te faisoit vivre;

Meurs, meurs donc, c'est trop lanterner,
Lors on entendit bourdonner,
Son esprit sortant de sa plaie:
Je ne sai si la chose est vraie.
Didon mourut, Iris s'enfuit,
Adieu, bon soir, et bonne nuit.[1]

Today it seems a shameless but consistently amusing defla-
tion of a great work. At the time it embraced a further and
more serious intention. It was a protest against pompous
writing. Scoffing at Vergil, it also cocked a snook at preciosity.
It purposely accepted the little eight-syllabled Italian line as a
contrast to the heavy measures of classical French writers. It
gave offence. It was meant to give offence. It was criticism.

It was the period of the anti-Mazarin campaign. The form
was admirably suited to political controversial abuse, and the
new vehicle of denigration swept the country. Naudé in his
Mascurat required a whole volume for the consideration of
burlesque published during only three months of the year 1649.
Not only did everyone write burlesque, but publishers, either
from ignorance or guile, added the description to all kinds of
publication—"d'ou vient que durant la guerre de Paris en
1649, on imprima une pièce assez mauvaise, mais sérieuse
pourtant avec ce titre qui fit justement horreur à tous ceux qui
n'en lurent pas davantage, *La Passion de Notre-Seigneur en vers
Burlesques*".[2] No doubt it had been sufficient for the publisher
that the poem was in the same metre and rhyming system as
the *Vergile Travesti*.

This devotion of a whole nation to a single variety of laughter
resulted in the swift deterioration of the joke. The more serious
writers grew wearied and irritated by the interminable facetiousness. A worthy priest, Father Vavasseur, wrote an enormous
book in Latin (1658) to prove that burlesque must be wrong
because none of the ancients used it.[3] Boileau who "read the
Burlesque Poetry of Scarron, with some kind of Indignation, as
witty as it was",[4] attacked it in his *Art Poétique*—and with the

---

[1] End of Book IV.
[2] Pellison-Fontanier. *Histoire de l'Académie Française,*
[3] *Francisci Vavassoris Societ. Iesu De Ludicra Dictione Liber In Quo Tota Jocandi
Ratio Ex Veterum Scriptis Aestimatur.*
[4] Dryden: *Discourse concerning the Original and Progress of Satire*, 1693.

publication of *Le Lutrin* in 1674, promoted the alternative laughter of the mock-heroic poem.

Burlesque in France was stunted in its youth by a surfeit of laughter. In England, though strongly influenced both by Scarron and Boileau, it was to grow up into an adult and peculiarly English joke. Samuel Butler was as powerful an influence as Scarron. Boileau was imitated by an equal artist in Alexander Pope. Burlesque became an original influence in the creation of the English novel: it established itself in splendour in the English theatre.

Speeded no doubt by Royalist connections with France and by the new liberties of 1660, the new joke was quickly accepted in England.[1] The first certain appearance of "burlesque" in English is in Blount's *Glossographia* in 1656, where it was defined as "drolish, merry, pleasant". In the following year, 1657, Pellison's *Histoire de l'Académie Française* (1653), which contained the reference to burlesque already quoted,[2] was published in English. Flecknoe's *Diarum* appeared in the same year: it advertised itself as being in "Burlesque Rhime, or Drolling Verse", and referred in its preface to Aristophanes, Plautus, Cervantes, Scarron and Tassoni.

The first part of Samuel Butler's *Hudibras* appeared in 1663, and in the same year Sir William Davenant's medley *The Play-house to be Lett*[3] proved that burlesque was sufficiently new to furnish a fashionable joke in the theatre.

In the first act, the Poet, who is one of those who wants to hire the play-house, explains himself thus:

POET: What think you
                    Of Romances travesti?
PLAYER: Explain you(r)self.
POET: The garments of our Fathers you must wear
                    The wrong side outward, and in time it may
                    Become a fashion.

---

[1] The origins and nature of English burlesque verse have been recorded by Richmond P. Bond in *English Burlesque Poetry 1700–1750* (1932). A feature of this valuable book is a "Register of Burlesque Poems" in which 211 works published between 1700 and 1750 are listed and described.

[2] See p. 20.

[3] First published 1673. See also pp. 29–31.

HOUSEKEEPER: It will be strange, and then 'tis sure to take.
POET: You shall present the actions of the Heroes
               (Which are the chiefest Theams of Tragedy)
               In Verse Burlesque.
PLAYER: Burlesque and Travesti? These are hard words,
               And may be *French*, but not Law French.

In 1664 came the second part of *Hudibras*,[1] and also Charles
Cotton's *Scarronides: or Virgile Travestie*, which though not
actually a translation of the work of Scarron was obviously
copied from it. This is Cotton's version of the same passage as
that just quoted from Scarron:

> At the Command of Heaven's Goddess
> She ties these Wings fast to her Boddice,
> Which waving did adorn the Sky
> With all the fair Variety
> Of colours that the Rainbow shows,
> When clad in her most gaudy Cloaths.
> Full swift she flew, till, coming near
> *Carthage*, she made a Chancelleer,
> And then a Stoop, when, having spy'd
> Queen Dido's Window staring wide
> Set open, you may well presume,
> (As there was Cause) to air the Room,
> She nimbly, to all Folks Amazement,
> Whips like a swallow through the Casement.
> O'er Dido's Head she took her Stand,
> And cries, whilst flourishing a Brand,
> Sent down from Juno Queen come I,
> Epilogue to this Tragedy;
> And thus, O Dido, set thee loose
> From Twitch of suffocating Noose.
> Which said, and tossing high her Blade
> With great Dexterity, the Maid,
> O wonderful! ev'n at one side-blow
> Spoil'd a good Rope, and down dropped Dido.

Cotton, like Scarron, is easy reading, amusing, irreverent,
rude. Its success promoted a spate of classical travesties—many
more of Vergil, others of Homer, Ovid and Lucian. The
burlesque of Samuel Butler, though also influenced by Scarron,

---

[1] The third part was published in 1679.

was something wholly different from this. It was written in the same metre—that was so usual an arrangement that Dryden in his *Discourse concerning the Original and Progress of Satire* referred to "the sort of Verse which is called *Burlesque*, consisting of Eight Syllables, or Four Feet" [1]—but it was native English in design and its laughter was dedicated on altars nearer home than the groves of classical Italy and Greece. It was less facetious and more witty than the classical travesty. It scoffed not at heroes but at puritans, and with a unique mixture of flippancy and satire. Because it was a topical composition much of its meaning is veiled from the modern reader, but parts of it are still as shiningly to the point as though they had been written about the troubles of the present age.

> For his religion, it was fit
> To match his learning and his wit:
> 'Twas Presbyterian true blue,
> For he was of that stubborn crew
> Of errant saints, whom all men grant
> To be the true church militant;
> Such as do build their faith upon
> The holy text of pike and gun;
> Decide all controversies by
> Infallible artillery;
> And prove their doctrine orthodox
> By apostolic blows and knocks;
> Call fire and sword, and desolation,
> A godly thorough reformation,
> Which always must be carried on,
> And still be doing, never done;
> As if religion were intended
> For nothing else but to be mended.

There was no comparable purpose in the burlesque of Cotton. Entirely concerned with debasing the unoffending great, Cotton's was a snickering kind of laughter, entertaining only so long as it shocked by its irreverence and surprised by its competence. In England, as in France, critical voices were soon raised against it.

In his translation (1683) of Boileau's *Art Poétique*, Sir William

---

[1] 1693. Wycherley's *Hero and Leander in Burlesque*, published 1669, is in five foot heroic couplets.

Soame, with Dryden's collaboration, fitted the French con-
demnation of burlesque with English examples.

> The dull Burlesque appear'd with impudence
> And pleas'd by Novelty, in Spite of Sence.
> All, except trivial points, grew out of date;
> *Parnassus* spoke the Cant of *Belinsgate*:
> Boundless and Mad, disordered Rhyme was seen:
> Disguised *Apollo* chang'd to *Harlequin* . . .
> But this low stuff the Town at last despis'd:
> And scorn'd the Folly that they once had pris'd;
> Distinguish'd Dull, from Natural and Plain,
> And left the villages to Fleckno's Reign.
> Let not so mean a style your Muse debase;
> But learn from Butler the Buffooning grace:
> And let Burlesque in Ballads be employ'd
> Yet noisy Bumbast carefully avoid.

Sir William Temple protested that "the Design, the Custom,
and Example are very pernicious to Poetry, and indeed to all
Virtue and Good Qualities among Men, which must be dis-
heartened by finding how unjustly and undistinguished they
fall under the lash of Raillery, and this Vein of Ridiculing the
Good as well as the Ill, the Guilty and the Innocent together."[1]
Dryden disliked the comic double rhymes of burlesque for
the solemn reason that "it turns Earnest too much to Jest, and
gives us a Boyish kind of Pleasure". And he had technical
objections. The eight-syllable line was too short. "When the
Rhyme comes too thick upon us, it streightens the Expression;
we are thinking of the Close, when we should be employ'd in
adorning the Thought."[2]
Boileau, in his mock-heroic poem *Le Lutrin* (1674) had proposed a different joke—the enlargement of the low, the devotion
to an unimportant theme of the machinery and solemnity of
epic poetry. Founded in imitation and decorated with parody,
it was a style of humour particularly well suited to English wit,
and in England it was to be brought to a pinacle of art beyond
anything that was in the nature of travesty to achieve. *Mac-
Flecknoe* (1682), *The Dispensary* (1699), *The Rape of the Lock*
(1712) and *The Dunciad* (1728) set the fashion and the form for

---

[1] "Of Poetry": *Miscellanea,* Second Part, 1690.
[2] *Discourse concerning the Original and Progress of Satire,* 1693.

the mock-heroic poetry of the 18th century, in which small themes—a doctor's quarrel, a lady's curl, bathos itself—were dignified by all the apparatus of classical poetry, little disputes described as largely as Olympian struggles, and parlour games treated as seriously as the sport of heroes.

The original octosyllabic burlesque verse—whether the travesty or the Hudibrastic type—was in strong decline by 1750 and barely outlasted the century. The mock-heroic remained popular much longer, but although the best poems of this type are still enjoyed, it is not often in the 20th century that anybody writes them. Rare examples are Hilaire Belloc's Newdigate poem on "*The Benefits of the Electric Light*", and the lines from an imaginary *Cacohymniad* printed as a proem to *The Stuffed Owl* (1930), an anthology of bad verse collected by D. B. Wyndham Lewis and Charles Lee.

> . . . She comes! She comes! Like castanets of Spain,
> Clip-clop, clip-clop, her slippers strike the plain,
> While from her lips proceeds th' oracular hum:
> "De-dum, de-dum, de-dumpty, dum-de-dum."
> A gander limps with outstretch'd neck before her,
> And owls and jays and cuckoos hover o'er her.
> Brisk at her elbow NAMBY PAMBY skips,
> Checking her chant on quiv'ring finger-tips;
> And close behind, strutting in laurell'd state,
> See! AUSTIN arm in arm with PYE and TATE. . . .

That the direct parody should continue in good health long after the dissolution of these sister arts is natural. Classical travesty was a static sort of humour. It made no progress in laughter; its materials were limited and soon exhausted. The mock-heroic admitted infinitely greater ingenuity, but it postulated a classical education both in the writer and in the reader. The parody is not bound by a fixed form of humour or by a particular kind of understanding. It is wholly free, and since each generation provides its own eccentricities of fashion, its materials are inexhaustible.

*   *   *   *   *

This long introduction to the subject of burlesque in the English theatre after 1660 has been necessary, first, because it

was essential to distinguish between satire, parody, and burlesque; second, because the book would have been incomplete
without some indication of the earlier burlesque in the theatre;
and third, because it is impossible to discuss burlesque at all
without considering the beginnings of the burlesque poem.

1660 has been chosen as the starting place for this study,
because it was at the Restoration that the high fashion for
burlesque was imported from France, and because the hot
spirits of the Restoration theatre provided exactly the right
atmosphere for the cultivation of the joke. As Ronald Knox has
written in his *Essays in Satire*, "It is . . . when good-humoured
men pick up this weapon of laughter, and, having no vendettas
to work off with it, begin idly tossing it at a mark, that humour
without satire takes its origin." Early burlesque, laced with
satire, and inspired by personal animosities, had often been
extremely savage. After *The Rehearsal* of 1671, the laughter
which was excited by rhymed couplets, bad verse, the Italian
opera, Augustan tragedy, the sentimental drama, the tale of
terror, the melodrama, the jolly jack tar, the Pre-Raphaelites,
and the Edwardian problem play, was increasingly good-
natured.

PART TWO

THE BURLESQUE TRADITION
IN
THE ENGLISH THEATRE
AFTER 1660

DAVENANT AND BUCKINGHAM

BURLESQUE had existed in the Elizabethan theatre as an ingredient of comedy. After 1660 it appears increasingly as a complete undertaking. It was introduced to the Restoration stage by the nimble Sir William Davenant, who had written masques for the Court and plays for the theatre before the Civil War, and had obtained in 1639 a patent from Charles I to build a theatre. In 1641 he fled to France, returned in 1642, was knighted at the siege of Gloucester in 1643, and returned to France after Marston Moor in 1644; there he served Queen Henrietta Maria, witnessed French entertainments, and became acquainted with the French fashion for travesty. Acting for the Queen as a messenger to England, he was captured at sea in 1650, confined in the Tower and nearly condemned to death—in spite of which, during the last four years of the Puritan ban against the theatre, he was permitted to organize certain musical entertainments in London, and, after 1660, succeeded, as of right, to the leading position in the Restoration theatre.

The first stage burlesque to claim the name 'burlesque' was included in Davenant's mixed entertainment, *The Play-house to be Lett*, produced at Lincoln's Inn Fields in 1663.

In the first act of the play several persons offer to hire the vacant playhouse. A poet is prepared to produce a work in Verse Burlesque.

> If I agree with you in finding your
> Disease, it is some sign that I may know
> Your remedy; which is the Travesti,
> I mean Burlesque, or more t' explain myself,
> Would say, the Mock-heroique must be it
> Which draws the pleasant hither i' the Vacation,
> Men of no malice who will pay for laughter.

"The pleasant". "Men of no malice". It is interesting to find Davenant differentiating at once between the laughter of satire and the laughter of burlesque.

Acts 2–5 are devoted to the different productions of the various applicants. Act 5 is provided by

> our *Bullies* the Burlesquers,
> That show the wrong side of the Hero's outward.

Their play is a burlesque on the Cleopatra story, and it is curious, first, because it is a stage presentation of the literary fashion for classical travesty, rather than a burlesque of any particular contemporary plays; secondly, because it was produced a year previous to the publication of Charles Cotton's *Scarronides or Virgile Travestie*; and thirdly because it was written in five foot heroic couplets at a moment when travesty was habitually written in four foot lines. Beaumont had made fun of the theatrical rhymed couplet years before in *The Knight of the Burning Pestle*. Davenant now made it the basis of his entire burlesque. It was the first step in the creation of the mock heroic play.

Act 5 of *The Play-house to be Lett* consists in that elementary form of burlesque, the farcical treatment of a classical subject. It is raw stuff, entirely written in feminine rhyming couplets (the device for laughter which Dryden so much disliked, because it "gives us a Boyish kind of Pleasure"). But the double rhyme is always good for a laugh and it comes off well enough to suggest that the play was highly diverting when the joke was new.

EUNUCH: Ah fickle fortune! who would e're have dreamt this,
           Rome's roaring Boys will swagger now at *Memphis*.
NIMPHIDIUS: Behold they come who quickly can inform us.
EUNUCH: *Nimphidius*, mum, be silent as a Dormouse.

Davenant has another connection with the early use of the word burlesque. His first play *The Witts* had been performed and published in 1634. There was nothing about burlesque in it then: nor when it was re-printed in 1665. But when Pepys saw the play in 1667 he reported it as "now corrected and enlarged", and when the play was published in the collected works in 1673, after Davenant's death, a catch was among the additions in the last act, followed by a stage direction, "The second catch is sung and acted by them in Recitative Burlesque".

The burlesque in *The Play-house to be Lett* did not laugh at the fashion for classical travesty. It made use of it. It was a dramatization of travesty, and was not more critical than the travesty itself. *The Rehearsal* by the Duke of Buckingham, produced at the Theatre Royal, Drury Lane, on December 7, 1671,[1] professed an entirely different intention. It was an attack upon contemporary writers—among others on the Howards, Sir Robert Stapylton, Orrery, Thomas Porter, Davenant, and, in chief, upon Dryden. This prodigiously successful play had too much of personal enmity in it to be a completely burlesque work. Its conception was burlesque, but its execution was something more fierce. Buckingham was out to scarify. The work is laced with direct parody and nowhere in the whole work is there the smallest suggestion of a lurking affection for the objects of the joke.

The history of burlesque in the theatre is the history of the evolution of laughter, from the distortion of malignity to the distortion of high spirits, from the wish to kill to the wish to preserve for laughter's sake. *The Rehearsal* was revived again and again during the 18th century and *The Critic* (1779) is directly derived from it; but *The Critic* is also the flower of a hundred years of burlesque development through the work of men like Gay, Fielding, and Henry Carey. The importance of *The Rehearsal* is therefore twofold. As critical parody it is established. It is equally important as the fount and origin of that procession of 18th century jokes, in which the tradition of English theatrical burlesque was gradually built up.

The beginning of Act 2 of *The Rehearsal* is a particularly good example of traditional burlesque. Having greeted each other, the Physician opens his conversation with the Court Usher with the words: "Sir, to conclude." "What, before he begins?" asks Smith, one of the visitors at the rehearsal. "No, sir," replies

---

[1] An earlier draft had been ready in 1665, but was withheld from performance by the closing of the theatres on account of the plague. Montague Summers' edition of *The Rehearsal* (1914) gives a full account of its origins, and detailed notes on the parodies.

Bayes. "You must know, they had been talking of this a pretty while without." This unwinking nonsense, which owes nothing to direct parody, is the very marrow of burlesque and the origin of a long pedigree of similar witticisms. Fielding has a parallel joke in *Pasquin* (1736) and Sheridan adapted it for the opening lines of Puff's play, *The Spanish Armada*.

SIR CHRISTOPHER HATTON: True, gallant Raleigh!
DANGLE: What, they had been talking before?
PUFF: O yes; all the way as they came along.

There is a fine burlesque joke of the same kind in Act 5 Scene 1 of *The Rehearsal*.

JOHNSON: But Mr. *Bayes*, did not you promise us just now, to make
         Amarillis speak very well?
BAYES: Ay, and so she would have done but that they hinder'd
         her.

Fielding improved upon this in the Ghost's speech in *Pasquin*.

>   From the dark Regions of the Realms below
>   The Ghost of Tragedy has ridden Post;
>   To tell thee, *Common Sense*, a thousand things,
>   Which do import thee nearly to attend;
>   [*Cock crows.*
>   But ha! the cursed Cock has warn'd me hence;
>   I did set out too late, and therefore must
>   Leave all my Business to some other time.
>   [*Ghost descends.*

Then Sheridan took the joke over, and turned it inside out in the Beefeater's soliloquy.

>   Though hopeless Love finds comfort in Despair
>   It never can endure a Rival's Bliss!
>   But soft—I am observed.
>   [*Exit.*

"That's a very short soliloquy," remarks Dangle. "Yes," replies Puff—"but it would have been a great deal longer if he had not been observed."

Imperfect logic, cultured obtuseness, the solemn defence of the non-sequitur: these are jokes which lie at the foundations of English burlesque. They turn up again and again and they are always good. Gaffer Goggles, for instance, in a forgotten

Victorian burlesque, *Briganzio the Brigand*,[1] is only creating a new variant upon the original joke.

> . . . I am the oldest inhabitant of this place.
> For four score years I've lived in that there cottage
> Yet never can my memory recall
> Finer ⎱
> Worse ⎰ weather than we've had this week.
> But hush! My daughter comes—I must dissemble.

The Physician's speech in *The Rehearsal*, "Sir, to conclude," continues with an engaging mixed metaphor of a storm "grasp'd but by the eye of reason"—and that again is a basic joke of burlesque—and then leads into a whispering scene, in which the author glances askew at a number of fatuous whisperings in contemporary dramas, but does not rely upon direct parody for the making of an admirable joke. The thing is irresistibly comic in itself.

PHYSICIAN: But yet some rumours great are stirring; and if *Lorenzo* should prove false (which none but the great Gods can tell) you then perhaps would find that—
　　　　　　　　　　　　　　　　　　　　　　　　[*Whispers.*

BAYES: Now he whispers.
USHER: Alone, do you say?
PHYSICIAN: No; attended with the noble—
　　　　　　　　　　　　　　　　　　　　　　　　[*Whispers.*

BAYES: Again.
USHER: Who, he in grey?
PHYSICIAN: Yes; and at the head of—
BAYES: Pray mark.
USHER: Then, Sir, most certain, 'twill in time appear. These are the reasons that have mov'd him to't; First, he—
　　　　　　　　　　　　　　　　　　　　　　　　[*Whispers.*

BAYES: Now the other whispers.
USHER: Secondly they—
　　　　　　　　　　　　　　　　　　　　　　　　[*Whispers.*

BAYES: At it still.
USHER: Thirdly, and lastly, both he and they—
　　　　　　　　　　　　　　　　　　　　　　　　[*Whispers.*

BAYES: Now they both whisper.
　　　　　　　　　　　　　　　　　　　[*Exeunt whispering.*

It may be that much of *The Rehearsal* would be unintelligible

[1] By Famars Hall, 1864(?).

to an audience today. But that particular joke of the confidential
opening is as fresh as when Buckingham first made it. Sheridan
used it, again turned about, in the magnificent 18th century
Elizabethan verse of Sir Walter Raleigh and Sir Christopher
Hatton.

SIR WALTER: You know, my Friend, scarce two revolving suns,
    And three revolving moons, have closed their course,
    Since Haughty Philip, in despight of Peace
    With hostile hand hath struck at England's Trade.
SIR CHRISTOPHER: I know it well.
SIR WALTER: Philip you know is proud Iberia's king!
SIR CHRISTOPHER: He is—
SIR WALTER: His subjects in base Bigotry
    And Catholic Oppression held—while we,
    You know, the Protestant Persuasion own—
SIR CHRISTOPHER: We do—
SIR WALTER: You know besides—his boasted Armament
    The famed Armada—by the Pope Baptized,
    With Purpose to invade these Realms—
SIR CHRISTOPHER: —Is sailed,
    Our last advices so report.
SIR WALTER: While the Iberian Admiral's chief hope,
    His darling son—
SIR CHRISTOPHER: Ferolo Wiskerandos hight—
SIR WALTER: The same—by chance a Prisoner hath been ta'en
    And in this fort of Tilbury—
SIR CHRISTOPHER: —Is now
    Confined—'tis true, and oft from yon tall turret's top
    I've marked the youthful Spaniard's haughty mien—
    Unconquer'd, tho' in chains.
SIR WALTER: You also know—
DANGLE: Mr. Puff, as he knows all this, why does Sir Walter go
    on telling him?

The relationship between the two scenes is obvious. But
Sheridan's is not just a repetition of Buckingham's joke. It adds
its own contribution to the building of the burlesque tradition.

The pedigree of the burlesque simile also springs from *The
Rehearsal*.

    So Boar and Sow, when any storm is nigh,
    Snuff up, and smell it gath'ring in the sky;

> Boar beckons Sow to trot in chestnut Groves,
> And there consummate their unfinish'd Loves:
> Pensive in mud they wallow all alone,
> And snore and gruntle to each others' moan.[1]

For two hundred and fifty years burlesque writers have continued to draw upon this joke. Fielding (less anxious than Buckingham to make a direct parody) specialized in it, and brought it to perfection in this passage in *Tom Thumb*.

> So have I seen some wild unsettled fool
> Who had her choice of this or that joint-stool;
> To give the preference to either loth,
> And fondly coveting to sit on both:
> While the two stools her sitting-part confound,
> Between 'em both falls squat upon the ground.

Later writers like Stevens and Rhodes carried the tradition, but with a smaller wit, into the 19th century. Even in the 20th century the joke has been preserved in *Savonarola Brown*.

Other famous jokes of burlesque recorded in *The Rehearsal* are Thunder and Lightning, the dance, the song, the ghost, [2] the bombastic hero[3]—and the ever agreeable joke of the two-man army.

1ST KING: What saucie Groom molests our privacies?
1ST HERALD: The Army's at the door, and in disguise,
           Desires a word with both your Majesties . . .

and later—

---

[1] The lines are a parody of a simile in *The Conquest of Granada*.

> So two kind turtles, when a storm is nigh,
> Look up, and see it gath'ring in the sky:
> Each calls his mate to shelter in the groves,
> Leaving, in murmurs, their unfinish'd loves:
> Perch'd on some dropping branch, they sit alone,
> And coo, and hearken to each other's moan.

Stevens in *Distress Upon Distress* (1752) borrows and fiddles with Buckingham's joke in the lines:

> In Straw-fill'd Sty, Thus have I heard a Swine
> Sigh for her Mate, for her Companion pine . . .

[2] The ghost, such a popular figure of future burlesques, is referred to, but not actually produced, in *The Rehearsal*.

[3] The bombastic hero is a very ancient joke. Bottom in the part of Pyramus antedates Drawcansir, hero of *The Rehearsal*, by three-quarters of a century.

BAYES: Wherefore, Sir, . . . I sum up my whole Battle in the representation of two persons only, no more: and yet so lively,
that, I vow to gad, you would swear ten thousand men were
at it really engag'd.

Buckingham's joke was verbal. Translated and developed
by Fielding and Sheridan [1] as a joke of properties and stage-
management, the two-man army and the ill-rehearsed battle
was to become a staple of burlesque, and to re-appear, fresh as
a daisy, in *Bombastes Furioso* (1810):—"Enter Bombastes,
attended by one Drummer, one Fifer, and two Soldiers, all very
materially differing in size".

Another joke rooted in *The Rehearsal* is the imperishable one
of the bad rhymed couplet. Buckingham was parodying the
heroic drama. The couplet was therefore essential to his
burlesque, and he has a final slap at it in the last lines of the
epilogue.

> Wherefore, for ours, and for the Kingdomes peace,
> May this prodigious way of writing cease.
> Let's have, at least, once in our lives, a time
> When we may hear some reasen, not all Rhyme:
> We have these ten years felt its Influence;
> Pray let this prove a year of Prose and Scence.

The petition was not granted. The great success of *The
Rehearsal* had no contrary effect upon the popularity either of
the heroic drama or of the heroic couplet. The rhymes went
on. But the couplet was subject to the entertaining literary
disease of bathos, and burlesque artists who came after Buckingham were to promote an extension of the joke—the cultivation
of bathos apart from direct parody, bathos for its own sake.
The vogue of the rhymed heroic tragedy—except for a few
isolated examples—did not last beyond 1680. But John Gay's
The What D'ye Call It (1715) was largely written in mock
heroics, and so in part are Fielding's *Tom Thumb* (1730–31),
Carey's *Chrononhotonthologos* (1733) and Stevens' *Distress upon
Distress* (1752). Carey's *The Dragon of Wantley* (1737) and *The
Dragoness* (1738), Stevens' *The Court of Alexander* (1770) and
Rhodes' *Bombastes Furioso* (1810) are wholly written in rhymed
couplets. It seemed that the couplet was accepted as a natural

----

[1] In *Pasquin, Tom Thumb, The Critic*.

medium for making nonsense of high sentiments: for which—besides the obvious natural glories of the thing—four reasons are evident. First, although rhymed tragedies were no longer written, the most eminent of those dramas still remained in the repertoire. Second, although the poets had given up writing rhymed tragedy, they still went on writing monstrous epics in rhymed verse; Pope made them the object of his great prose burlesque, *The Art of Sinking* by Martinus Scriblerus (published in 1728). Third, the rhymed couplet was the accepted form for mock-heroic poetry.[1] Fourth, the joke was kept fresh in the mind by the continued prestige and frequent performance of *The Rehearsal*.

From the burlesques of the 18th century the couplet was inherited by the 19th century extravaganza, which in part [2] bequeathed it to the pantomime, where it still lingers. The man who writes today a burlesque couplet for a demon king is following a tradition, which can be traced through Henry J. Byron, J. R. Planché, W. B. Rhodes, G. R. Stevens, Henry Carey, Henry Fielding, John Gay, Alexander Pope, and many lesser writers, to the beginnings of the burlesque couplet in Buckingham's *Rehearsal*, and Davenant's *The Play-house to be Lett*. The joke of the bathos, of the sudden fall, is as ever welcome as the joke of that other sudden fall when the fat man slips on the banana skin. It is a fundamental joke.

The 17th and 18th centuries were more fortunate than the 19th and 20th. They had models for their pleasure—poets like Aaron Hill, whose poem on The Creation contains the following engaging passage upon fish:

> Warm and gay, the nimbler kind
> Upward roll, the top to find,
> And, leaping, cool their livers in the wind.

Lord Hervey, who propounded the engrossing question,

> Will the wise elephant desert the wood,
> To imitate the whale and range the flood?
> Or will the mole her native earth forsake
> In wanton madness to explore the lake?

---

[1] See pp. 26–7.
[2] In part, because the sung portions in earlier pantomimes were largely conducted in *serious* rhymed couplets.

and Sir Richard Blackmore, whose ponderous images are the
main ornament of *The Art of Sinking:*

> The finny tyrant of the spacious seas
> Shall send a scaly embassy for peace;
> His plighted faith the Crocodile shall keep,
> And seeing thee, for joy sincerely weep.

And dramatists, who, among great passages justly valued, could
nevertheless deliver themselves of such solemnities as these:—
From Orrery's *Mustapha* (1665)

ROXALANA: Will Heav'n more weight on our affliction lay?
HALY: Madam, the Guards and Train of *Mustapha*
          Assault the Camp with their united Force
          And are assisted by Prince *Zanger's* Horse.

From Banks' *The Rival Kings* (1677)

Tell her, some God, whiles slumber seals her Eyes,
How pitifully Oroondates lies;
That in kind feeling of the Tears I shed,
She come like *Thetis* to my wat'ry Bed.

From Elkana Settle's *The Empress of Morocco* (1673)

Sir, of your Progress a Relation make—
How died the King? How did the Poison take?

THOMAS DUFFETT

MENTION of *The Empress of Morocco* leads immediately to a
consideration of the solitary art of Thomas Duffett. Settle's play
was produced with immense success at the Duke's theatre in
July 1673.   In the following November a burlesque of the show
was produced at the Theatre Royal, together with a curious
"Epilogue, Being a new Fancy after the old, and most surprising way of Macbeth, Performed with new and costly
Machines"—which was a burlesque of the recent revival of the
Davenant version of *Macbeth*, which Pepys had praised in
1667 for its *"divertisement"*, and which John Downes had de-
scribed in 1671, "being drest in all its Finery, as . . . new Scenes,
Machines, as flyings for the Witches, with all the singing, and
Dancing in it . . . being in the nature of an Opera". In April

1674 the Duke's theatre presented Shadwell's operatic version of *The Tempest*. In the following November the Theatre Royal again produced a burlesque, *The Mock-Tempest*. In February 1675 Shadwell's *Psyche* was acted at the Duke's theatre. Three months later the Theatre Royal followed with *Psyche Debauch'd*.

All these burlesques, the work of one Thomas Duffett, deserve a closer inspection than they have hitherto received. Their literary merit is certainly small, but the light which they throw upon the works burlesqued is large. It is evident that the resources of the Duke's theatre were superior to those of the Theatre Royal, and that Duffett was quick to make a virtue of necessity by mocking at the scenery, machines and stage-effects of the other house. There had been some stage-managerial jokes in *The Rehearsal*—a burlesque of the machines in *Tyrannick Love*, for instance—but Buckingham never got as much fun out of stage business as Duffett was to do in these burlesques of 1673-5.

The burlesque of *The Empress of Morocco* is nothing, except for the interest which attaches to one of the stage-directions. "Enter King, Queen, &c., with Attendants; their Trains supported by Porters and Gypsies; a Heathen dance is presented by Tinkers and Jack puddings, who bring in an artificial broad spreading broom about which they dance to Drum-stick and Kettle, Tongs and Key, Morish, Timbrel and Saltbox etc." It is possible to understand the point of all that, because of the often reproduced picture from Settle's play illustrating his direction, "A Moorish Dance is presented by Moors in several Habits who bring in an artificial Palm-tree, about which they dance to several antick Instruments of Musick".[1]

The *Macbeth* epilogue was obviously something which had to be seen. First, Thunder and Lightning are discovered upon the stage in character. Then, "Three Witches fly over the Pit Riding upon Beesomes. *Heccate* descends over the Stage in a Glorious Charriot, Adorn'd with Pictures of Hell and Devils, and made of a large Wicker Basket." The witches describe their experiences, sing a health in praise of well-known bawds, perform spells, and then fly off amid thunder and lightning, singing

[1] This picture can be found on p. 224 of Allardyce Nicoll's *British Drama* (1925). A picture of William Harris as the Empress of Morocco in Duffett's burlesque is reproduced on p. 282 of *The Restoration Theatre* (1934) by Montague Summers.

a parody of a nursery rhyme. Buckingham had introduced
Thunder and Lightning as speaking characters in the prologue
to Mr. Bayes' play. Duffett's joke is different and is the father
of many developments, including the joke inverted, the failure
of effects, which Fielding included in *Pasquin* (1736).

FIREBRAND: Avert these omens, ye auspicious stars!
FUSTIAN: What omens? Where the devil is the thunder and
           lightning?
PROMPTER: Why don't you let go the thunder there and flash your
           rosin?
                                        [*Thunder and Lightning.*
FUSTIAN: Now Sir, begin if you please. I desire Sir, you will get a
           larger thunderbowl, and two pennyworth more of light-
           ning against the representation. Now, Sir, if you please.

Felicitous results may be obtained from the burlesque of
effects and it is likely that Duffett's *Macbeth* was both good fun
and good criticism. The final couplet suggests that he had the
right idea in his head.

> Since with success great Bards grow proud and resty;
> To get good Plays be kind to bad Travesty.

The *Mock-Tempest* was castigated by Sir William Soame and
Dryden in the translation of Boileau's *Art Poétique* published in
1683.

> . . . The dullest Scribblers some Admirers found,
> And the *Mock-Tempest* was a while renown'd:
> But this low stuff the Town at last despis'd:
> And scorn'd the Folly that they once had pris'd . . .

In his introduction to *The Rehearsal* (p. xxi), Montague
Summers quotes these lines as evidence that, even in their own
day, Duffett's burlesques were speedily forgotten. Surely the
correct deduction is precisely the opposite. This kind of burlesque is not long-lasting; that it should have been mentioned
ten years after its production is strong evidence that the joke
had been an effective one.[1]

The *Mock-Tempest* is a full length show, rather muddled and

[1] In *The Playhouse of Pepys* (1935) Montague Summers wrote of Duffett:
"He left a volume of Poems, two comedies, a masque, and three burlesques,
the merit of which is vastly underrated"—an important correction of the
opinion expressed in his edition of *The Rehearsal* (1914): "Coarse and puer-
ile, Duffett's farces fully deserve the oblivion into which they have fallen."

considerably rude. But it is not without humour. And, as in the other show, much point is made about the scenic effects of the original production.

PROSPERO; Well, *Ariel* go let a table be brought to them furnish'd with most sumptuous Cates, but when they try to eat let two great Baboons be let down with ropes to snatch it away.

ARIEL: O Sir *Punchanello* did that at the Playhouse.

PROSPERO: Did he so—then bend thy ayry ear.

[*Whispers.*

ARIEL: More toyle—I pry'thee now let me mind thee of thy promise then—where is my Two-penny Custard?

Threats follow, as in the Shakespearean original, and Ariel gives way.

PROSPERO: Then do as I commanded, but make hast least the Conjurer of t'other House steal the Invention.

Psyche Debauch'd is the most elaborate and most intelligible of the three shows. Shadwell's opera is a prodigiously foolish piece, an elaborate solemnity full of processions and sacrifices and priests chanting litanies—

Jupiter, Juno, Minerva, Saturn, Cibele,
Be propitious to our vows and prayers.

To which Duffett replied with

2ND PRIEST: *James Naylor, Pope Joan, Wat Tyler, Moll Cutpurs, Chocorelly,*

ALL ANSWER: Help our Opera, because 'tis very Silly.

2ND PRIEST: *Hocus-pocus, Don Quixot, Jack Adams, Mary Ambry, Frier Bungy, William Lilly,*

ALL ANSWER: Help our Opera, because 'tis very Silly.

2ND PRIEST: *Carpentero, Paintero, Dancero, Musickero, Songstero, Punchanelly—*

ALL ANSWER: Help our Opera, because 'tis very Silly.

There is nothing clever about that. But anyone can see that it is funny; and that it would still be funny if it were put upon the stage today. The last of the invocations is another jab at the machines and scenery of the other theatre, which are burlesqued throughout the piece. The entry of Venus in a chariot drawn by doves is paralleled by the entry of a witch drawn by broomsticks: and much use is made of thunder and lightning, oracles, and every kind of sacerdotal nonsense. The prologue ends with these lines—

> Show some of your good Natures here kind Sirs;
> If our Conceit less proud or gay appears,
> She's less expensive, and more brisk than theirs.

Psyche Debauch'd marks the first important appearance of that famous burlesque character, the ghost. Jasper merely pretends to be a ghost in *The Knight of the Burning Pestle*, and in *The Rehearsal* the ghost is only mentioned incidentally. Duffett produced not only King Andrew's ghost *"Crown'd, and* Red-streak *with her head in her hand—attended with two Spirits"*, but three other ghosts besides.

The Rehearsal and *The Critic* were founded in verbal wit. The Duffett burlesques were founded in high spirits and visual wit. When the occasion was over, so was the piece. The plays are not important in the history of dramatic literature. They are important in the history of dramatic burlesque—important for two reasons. First, because they introduce a new idea: they are burlesques of one particular show—burlesques of the author, the actor, the carpenter, the dancer, the scene-painter, the prompter, the wardrobe, and the man on the ropes. Second, because they are conceived in great gaiety of spirit. The author does not appear to feel any grave responsibility to chastize. What he felt was a powerful impulsion to laugh; and that is the first element in burlesque which divides it from satire.

The burlesque of production can never be plainly translated to the printed page, but it occupies a high place in the burlesque tradition. Sheridan worked the joke at the end of *The Critic*, and everyone who saw the Old Vic production during 1945–6 knows how funny it can be. Original burlesque is not often seen in the theatre now—except in those skits of contemporary plays which sometimes appear in revues. These are directly in the Duffett tradition, the only difference being that the revue skit is potted, and the Duffett skits were made at considerable length.

In 1673—the year of Duffett's first skit—a comedy called *The Reformation*, by the Rev. Joseph Arrowsmith, was produced at the Duke's theatre. It contains a curious burlesque recipe for the making of a tragedy.

. . . I take a subject, as suppose the Siege of *Candy*, or the conquest of Flanders, and by the way Sir let it alwayes be some war-like action; you can't imagine what a grace a Drum and Trumpet give a Play. Then Sir I take you some three or four or half a dozen Kings, but most commonly two or three serve my turn, not a farthing matter whether they lived within a hundred years of one another . . . and let the Play be what it will, the Characters are still the same . . . As Sir you must alwayes have two Ladies in Love with one man, or two men in love with one woman; if you make them the Father and the Son, or two Brothers, or two Friends, 'twill do the better. There you know is opportunity for love and honour and Fighting, and all that . . . Then Sir you must have a Hero that shall fight with all the world: yes i'gad, and beat them too, and half the gods into the bargain if occasion serves . . . Last of all, be sure to raise a dancing singing ghost or two, court the Players for half a dozen new scenes and fine cloaths (for take me if there ben't much in that too) put your story into rime, and kill enough at the end of the Play, and *Probatum est* your business is done for Tragedy.

That 17th century pattern of humour was not to be developed further for some time. Duffett's last skit in 1675 had no successors. One reason for this was the temper of the times. Between 1680 and 1690 controversy was political and religious, not literary. A second reason may be found in the union of the two theatres between 1682 and 1695. The playhouse had no rival to criticize. A third reason lies in the fact that writers like Congreve, Mrs. Behn, Vanburgh, and George Farquhar, were providing different and successful kinds of laughter. Doubtless there was broad burlesque in the booths of Bartholomew Fair—but in the theatre the laughter of criticism was in need of new exercise. The 18th century was to provide it—in Italian opera, pantomime, the blank verse tragedy, classical, Augustan, or domestic, and, later, in the finest of all gifts to laughter, the sentimental drama.

JOHN GAY

IN the preface to *The What D'ye Call It* (1715) "a tragi-comi-pastoral farce", John Gay claims to be "the first who have introduced this kind of Dramatick entertainment upon the stage": and although that was written as part of a mock learned examination of the play, it is not the less true. Forty years had gone by since the burlesques of Thomas Duffett, and no development in the practice of stage burlesque had been made in all that time. Gay was making a new start—and much as burlesque in the theatre owes to Buckingham, it must be remembered that it derives even more from the heroic plays, whether in rhyme or not, which came later than his disciplining.[1] The oaths, the rants of love and honour, the mad scenes and the ghosts—all the extravagances of Lee, Crowne, Banks, Otway and Settle—had created a new source of burlesque material. Gay is what he claimed to be—an original. He is important, because he first made use of this new store of laughter; because he had the wit to preserve the rhymed couplet; because he developed the joke of putting high sentiments into the mouths of the low—an essential characteristic of travesty and burlesque poetry, but not a main point in the burlesque of Buckingham; because he maintained the ghost (indeed five of them[2]); and because he set a new standard by developing the idea of general burlesque.

Perhaps one should not say 'he'. *The What D'ye Call It* was a fruit of that great combination of wits, the Scriblerus Club. Any of them—Swift, Arbuthnot, Pope, Parnell, or Oxford—may have had a hand in it, and Pope almost certainly did. Some of the allusions in the play are obscure, but the public was not left long in ignorance of their meaning. Within six weeks of the first performance (February 23, 1714/15) *A Complete Key* was published together with a *Hypercritical Preface on the Nature of Burlesque, and the Poet's Design*—an excellent jest, which was generally believed to be the work of the authors themselves.

The Complete Key praises His Grace of Buckingham for laying his finger on the proper subjects of ridicule, and objects that this "odd-contriv'd" *What D'ye Call It* "seems rather to be a Banter on the solemn stile of Tragedy, in general, than a Satyr

---

[1] Five editions of *The Rehearsal* were published in Buckingham's lifetime, but the third edition, published in 1675 was the last to contain alterations. The fourth (1683) and fifth (1687) though claiming "Amendments and large Additions" were only re-issues of the third edition.

[2] "A dancing singing ghost or two" is mentioned in Arrowsmith's *The Reformation* (see p. 43). Gay's ghosts are dancers and singers.

upon faulty Passages in our Poets."[1] This is concealed praise.
It is precisely because it was not tied to parody that Gay's joke
is more flexible than Buckingham's. *The What D'ye Call It* contains parody—but the play is more than a collection of parodies,
more than a collection of burlesque situations. The piece has
been conceived as a general burlesque of style, and for that
reason it is nearer to Sheridan, Beerbohm or Leacock than it
is to Buckingham. *The What D'ye Call It*, like *The Critic*,
is wholly intelligible to a modern audience. *The Rehearsal* is
not.[2]

Finally, and most important, Gay introduced the beginnings
of that sobriety which is the essential ingredient of the best
humour. *The What D'ye Call It* is full of admirable nonsense
fitted for grave delivery—and it is on record that the piece was
originally performed with calculated restraint. Dr. Johnson in
his *Life of John Gay* speaks of *The What D'ye Call It* as "a kind
of mock-tragedy, in which the images were comick, and the
action grave; so that, as Pope relates, Mr. Cromwell, who could
not hear what was said, was at a loss how to reconcile the
laughter of the audience with the solemnity of the scene."

KITTY: When gentlefolks their sweethearts leave behind,
          They can write letters, and say something kind;
          But how shall *Filbert* unto me indite,
          When neither I can read, nor he can write?
          Yet, Justices, permit us ere we part
          To break this nine-pence, as you've broke our heart.
                              [*Breaking the ninepence.*
FILBERT: As this divides, thus are we torn in twain.
                              [*Joining the pieces.*

[1] Allardyce Nicoll seems as puzzled by the play as the authors of *A Complete Key* pretended to be. They call it "odd-contriv'd": he calls it "peculiar" on no less than five occasions in *British Drama* (1925) and *A History of
Early 18th Century Drama*, (1925). To some it may seem peculiar that Professor Nicoll should class this palpable burlesque as a sentimental comedy.
But the identical mistake was made at the original production by the people
of the pit and gallery, who (according to Alexander Pope) "received it at
first with great gravity and sedateness, some few with tears; but after the
third day they also took the hint, and have ever since been very loud in
their claps."
[2] The Cambridge Marlowe Society gave a memorable performance of
The What D'ye Call It in 1920.

KITTY: And as this meets, thus may we meet again.
          [*She is drawn away on one side of the Stage by* AUNT
          and GRANDMOTHER.
          Yet one look more—
FILBERT (*Haul'd off on the other side by the* SERJEANT):
                    —One more ere yet we go.
KITTY: To part is death.—
FILBERT: —'Tis death to part.
KITTY: —Ah!
FILBERT: —Oh!

Fielding was so impressed by this pleasantry that he carried
it over into *Tom Thumb*.

GLUMDALCA: Ah Wretched Queen!
KING: Oh! Wretched King!
GLUMDALCA: Ah!
KING: Oh![1]

Kitty's distracted speech, after her lover has been sent for a
soldier, is beautifully written. It is not tilting at anybody in
particular. It is funny because of its own wide-eyed simplicity,
its planned fatuity.

KITTY: Dear happy fields, farewell: ye flocks, and you
       Sweet meadows, glitt'ring with the pearly dew:
       And thou, my rake, companion of my cares,
       Giv'n by my mother in my younger years:
       With thee the toils of full eight springs I've known,
       'Tis to thy help I owe this hat and gown:
       On thee I lean'd, forgetful of my work,
       While *Tom* gaz'd on me, propt upon his fork:
       Farewell, farewell; for all thy task is o'er,
       Kitty shall want thy service now no more.
                                [*Flings away the rake.*

Later Kitty has a mad speech—an early example of a joke
which was to become popular later.

GRANDMOTHER: She swoons, poor soul—help *Dolly*.
AUNT: —She's in fits.
       Bring water, water, water.—   [*Screaming.*

---

[1] For some curious reason, Fielding, in the notes, attributes *The What
D'ye Call It* line to *Don Carlos*—as though he had been burlesquing a real
tragedy line and not borrowing from Gay.

GRANDMOTHER: —Fetch her wits.

[They throw water upon her.

KITTY: Hah!—I am turned a stream—look all below;
It flows, and flows, and will for ever flow.
The meads are all afloat—the haycocks swim.
Hah! who comes here!—my *Filbert!* Drown not him.
Bagpipes in butter, flocks in fleecy fountains,
Churns, sheep-hooks, seas of milk, and honey-mountains.

Here Gay is parodying Dryden and Otway—particularly Otway's

Murmuring Streams, soft Shades, and spring Flowers.
Lutes, Lawrels, Seas of Milk, and Ships of Amber,

from *Venice Preserv'd*—but one does not feel, as one does with the parodies in *The Rehearsal,* that a rival author has been publicly insulted. Kitty's speech is funny for its own sake. Burlesque is exercising its best function—laughing for pleasure, not laughing to hurt.

The Beggar's Opera (1728) is a different matter. This famous and remarkable work wears four faces. It is a satire on low life, a satire on high life, a satire on government—and a burlesque of the Italian opera.

The opera had edged its way into the English theatre during 1705-9 in pieces derived from the Italian, but sung usually in English.[1] It very quickly attracted the laughter of *The Tatler, The Spectator,* and of the side-shows at the Fairs. Mrs. Delany, who was born in 1700, has recorded that she saw as a child "Powell's famous puppet show, in which Punch fought with a pig in burlesque, in imitation of Nicolini's battle with the lion. My lord Bolingbroke was of the party, and made me sit upon his lap to see it." [2] Nicolini came to England in 1708. The

[1] *Gay's Beggar's Opera, its Content, History and Influence* by W. E. Schultz (1923) contains a valuable chapter on Gay's burlesque of the Italian opera. See also Allardyce Nicoll's *History of Early 18th Century Drama* (1925) for an account of the Italian opera in London (p. 225) and a list (p. 387) showing the prodigious number of Italian works performed in the first half of the century. The list in his *History of Late 18th Century Drama* (p. 348) is even longer. See also *Memoirs of the Musical Drama* by George Hogarth (1838).

[2] See *The Autobiography and Correspondence of Mary Granville, Mrs. Delany,* edited by Lady Llanover (1861), Vol. 1, p. 16.

absurd but highly successful opera, in which he fought with the lion, was *Hydaspes*, and Mrs. Delany's visit to the puppet show must have been not long after the opera's production at the Haymarket on 23rd March, 1710.

On the London stage the Italian opera had already been burlesqued by Richard Estcourt as early as 1708, in *Prunella*, one song in which—

> Bring me the Bottle
> Who dares oppose him?
> The Spleen and Vapours
> Before him fly——

will be recognized as a skit on the still popular aria, "Love leads to battle", by Buononcini.

Other burlesques followed. In 1716 at Lincoln's Inn Fields, Richard Leveridge twisted a rehearsal play out of " Pyramus and Thisbe" in *A Midsummer Night's Dream*, making "bold to dress out the original in Recitative and Airs after the present Italian mode", with Semibreve, Crochet and Gamut taking the places of Shakespeare's courtiers. Leveridge called his piece *The Comick Masque of Pyramus and Thisbe*, but it is no masque in the correct sense of the word and Allardyce Nicoll wrongly lists it as one. With good comic music *Pyramus and Thisbe* must have made an excellent burlesque opera. "This is the most Musical Partition I ever heard," says Gamut after a song by Wall. And, when Pyramus dies, singing, Crochet observes, "I'll assure you the man died well, like a Hero in an Italian Opera to very good Time and Tune".

In 1708 *Pyrrhus & Demetrius* had been performed by English and Italian singers, each singing in his own language: but from January 1710 the opera was performed in Italian—greatly to the satisfaction of the world of fashion, and greatly to the disgust of the English authors and actors. Uncomplimentary references to the opera and to its performers are to be found in countless essays, poems, prologues and plays [1]—and not only in the early years of the invasion. At a much later date Mrs. Kitty Clive could remark with customary vigour—"a set of Italian squalling

---

[1] E.g. *Harlequin Hydaspes* (1719), D'Urfey's *The Two Queens of Brentford* (1721), *The Contre Temps; or Rival Queans* (1727).

devils who come over to England to get our bread from us, and I say curse them all for a parcel of Italian bitches".[1]

The Italian opera was an object of jealousy. It was also (and has ever remained) a sweet subject for burlesque. It is hardly to be supposed therefore that the original *Beggar's Opera* was quite such a pretty charming thing as the 20th century has made it.[2] Something has been lost. The present day playgoer no longer identifies the quarrel of Walpole and Townshend with the quarrel of Peachum and Lockit, and "Robin of Bagshot, *alias* Gorgon, *alias* Bluff Bob, *alias* Carbuncle, *alias* Bob Booty" remains a good joke for a multitude who fail to recognize in it a series of abuses against Sir Robert. Today only the satire of Society is still discernible; the satire upon government must be discovered by the curious; and the burlesque of the Italian singers has been wholly obscured by the success of the ballad opera form, and subsequently of the comic opera. The fact is that after two hundred years of English light opera, the 20th century is no longer qualified to recognize the extent of Gay's original burlesque. Even his bare-faced contrivance for a happy ending passes unnoticed in a world educated to the inanities of musical comedy.

Some critics, and one at least in the 18th century,[3] have professed themselves unable to perceive any burlesque of the Italian singers in *The Beggar's Opera*. The hit was plain enough to the audiences of 1728. Mrs. Pendarves (afterwards Mrs. Delany)

---

[1] Tate Wilkinson *Memoirs* (1790) Vol. 2, p. 29. Tate Wilkinson, referring to a performance of *Thomas & Sally* in 1762, makes the doubly unexpected remark, "I acted Dorcas as an Italian". *Ibid.*, Vol. 3, p. 93.

[2] A method of production wholly contrary to Nigel Playfair's was several times inflicted on the public in the last quarter of the 18th century by the two George Colmans. In their *Beggar's Opera Reversed* women played the men's parts, and the men the women's. Gay's *Achilles* was also 'reversed' by George Colman the Elder as *Achilles in Petticoats*. On the occasion of Dowton's benefit in 1817 even *The Rivals* suffered reversal—presumably to give Dowton the fun of playing Mrs. Malaprop.

In the first year of its history *The Beggar's Opera* was played in Dublin with a cast of children, none of them above ten years old. Peg Woffington played Polly. Only four years later she made her first appearance in London as Macheath. Even so late as 1829 a craze for oddities permitted Harriet Coveney to appear as Macheath at an age of less than fourteen. The part was often played by a woman—notably by Madame Vestris.

[3] Sir John Hawkins.

wrote to her sister, Ann Granville, almost immediately after the first performance, and used the very word. "Yesterday I was at the new opera composed by Handel; I like it extremely, but the taste of the town is so depraved, that nothing will be approved of but the burlesque. The Beggar's Opera entirely triumphs over the Italan one; I have not seen it, but everybody that has seen it, says it is very comical and full of humour . . ." [1] So the gossip went; and Swift, who knew the author's mind exactly, wrote roundly in *The Intelligencer* "This comedy likewise exposeth with great Justice, that unnatural Taste for Italian music among us, which is wholly unsuited to our northern climate, and the Genius of our people, whereby we are over-run with Italian effeminancy, and Italian nonsense."

Doubtless the burlesque was as much in the performance as in the text, but the Beggar's speech in the Prologue is a sufficient indication both of the nature and of the whereabouts of the hits against the Italians.

This Piece I own was originally writ for the celebrating the Marriage of *James Chanter* and *Moll Lay*, two most excellent Ballad-Singers. I have introduc'd all the Similies that are in all your celebrated *Operas*: The *Swallow*, the *Moth*, the *Bee*, the *Ship*, the *Flower*, etc. Besides I have a Prison Scene, which the Ladies always reckon charmingly pathetick. As to the Parts, I have observ'd such a nice Impartiality to our two Ladies that it is impossible for either of them to take Offence. [2] I hope I may be forgiven, that I have not made my Opera throughout unnatural, like those in vogue; for I have no Recitative: Excepting this, as I have consented to have neither Prologue nor Epilogue, it must be allow'd an Opera in all its forms.

Burlesque or not, it is certain that *The Beggar's Opera* acted the Italian opera off the stage. "The Opera will not survive

[1] See *The Autobiography and Correspondence of Mary Granville, Mrs. Delany*, Vol. 1, p. 158. *The Beggar's Opera* was first played on January 29th. The letter is dated January 19th, which must be a mistake. Possibly it was written on February 19th: internal evidence, to which Mr. Lawrence Tanner has drawn my attention, shows that it was certainly written after February 10th.

[2] The immediate reference was to the violent quarrel between the two Italian prima donnas, Cuzzoni and Faustina, in 1727. The light-hearted suggestion that no actress would quarrel about Polly and Lucy was disproved in 1736 by an equally bitter dispute on this very point between Mrs. Clive and Mrs. Cibber.

after this winter," wrote Mrs. Pendarves to her sister on February 29th; "I wish I were a poet worthy the honour of writing its elegy. I am certain excepting some few, the English have *no real taste for musick*; for if they had, they could not neglect an entertainment so perfect in its kind for a parcel of ballad singers."

HENRY FIELDING

WITHIN a few weeks of the first performance of *The Beggar's Opera* Henry Fielding's first play, *Love in Several Masques*, was performed at Drury Lane. He was not then twenty-one years old. He had begun to write in a bountiful period of English humour. Pope, Swift and Arbuthnot had long been compiling the mock-learned works of Martinus Scriblerus[1]; *Gulliver's Travels* was published in 1726; *The Art of Sinking* appeared in 1728; *The Dunciad* was re-published in a larger form in 1729. And in 1730, Fielding, still not twenty-three, was bold enough to produce and publish two burlesques under the pseudonym of Scriblerus Secundus, and, with learned notes and a pompous preface, to carry on and indeed to build upon his elders' wit. He had behind him the tradition of Buckingham and Gay: he had around him the new material offered by the rising crazes for opera and for harlequin, and by the 18th century development of blank verse tragedy: he was witness to the first beginnings of the modern novel: he had heard the first trumpetings of 18th century patriotism. He had an opportunity which had not arisen since the first performance of *The Rehearsal*.

Of Fielding's many works for the theatre five were important in the history of burlesque: *The Author's Farce* (1730); *Tom Thumb* (1730—enlarged 1731); *The Covent Garden Tragedy* (1732); *Pasquin* (1736); *Tumble Down Dick* (1736).

The Author's Farce in the main is what it claims to be—farce, satirical farce. But it is a rehearsal play, and when that part

---

[1] *Memoirs of the extraordinary Life, Works, and Discoveries of Martinus Scriblerus* were published in Pope's *Works* in 1741. The name Scriblerus was first used in print in *The Art of Sinking* (1728) and the variorum annotated edition of *The Dunciad* (1729). See the preface to *Memoirs . . . of Martinus Scriblerus*, ed. Charles Kerby-Miller (1950).

is reached, rather late, the manner changes. The play within the play is concerned with the election of an arch-poet for the service of the Goddess of Nonsense (which in itself is an obvious parallel with Pope's figure of Dulness in *The Dunciad*). Don Tragedio, Sir Farcical Comic, Dr. Orator, Signor Opera, Monsieur Pantomime and Mrs. Novel compete, and Opera is chosen. It is not good burlesque, for the spirit of the thing is at once too satirical and too knock-about: but it is interesting to see him working the new material.

> *The curtain drawn up to soft music, discovers the* GODDESS OF NONSENSE *on a throne.* . . .
>
> NONSENSE: Let all my votaries prepare
> To celebrate this joyful day.
> LUCKLESS: Gentlemen, observe what a lover of recitative Nonsense is.

The show ends with an early example of the "recognition" joke, with half the characters crying out "My wife!" "My sister!" "My daughter!" "My brother!" "My son!"

Tidied up, this joke was to appear in *The Critic* nearly fifty years later.

> [*Enter* JUSTICE'S LADY.
>
> LADY: Forgive this interruption, good my love;
> But as I just now pass'd a pris'ner youth,
> Whom rude hands hither lead,—strange bodings seiz'd
> My flutt'ring Heart, and to myself I said,
> An' if our Tom had liv'd he'd surely been
> This Stripling's Height!
> JUSTICE: Ha! sure some Powerful sympathy directs
> Us both—   [*Enter* SON *and* CONSTABLE.
> What is thy name?
> SON: My name's Tom Jenkins—*Alias* have I none;
> Though orphan'd, and without a Friend!
> JUSTICE: Thy parents?
> SON: My Father dwelt in Rochester—and was
> As I have heard—a Fishmonger—no more . . .
> LADY: How loudly Nature whispers to my Heart!
> Had he no other name?
> SON: I've seen a Bill
> Of his signed Tomkins, creditor.
> JUSTICE: This does indeed confirm
> Each circumstance the Gypsey told—Prepare!
> SON: I do.

JUSTICE: No Orphan, nor without a Friend, art thou—
           I am thy Father; here's thy Mother, there
           Thy uncle—this thy first cousin, and those
           Are all your near Relations.
LADY: O ecstasy of bliss!
SON: O most unlook'd for Happiness!
LADY: O wonderful event!   [*Faints.*

Another famous joke of burlesque had been established.
Nearly seventy years later it appears again, neatly turned about
in *Box and Cox*, (1847), by John Maddison Morton.

BOX: Cox! you'll excuse the apparent insanity of the remark, but
     the more I gaze on your features, the more I'm convinced that
     you're my long-lost brother.
COX: The very observation I was going to make to you.
BOX: Ah—tell me—in mercy tell me—have you such a thing as a
     strawberry mark on your left arm?
COX: No!
BOX: Then 'tis he!
                              [*They rush into each others' arms.*

In *Tom Thumb*, produced at the Little Theatre in the Haymarket within four weeks of *The Author's Farce*, Fielding set
aside the new jokes of opera and harlequin, and turned back
to burlesque tragedy.[1] It was an old joke, but Fielding's version
of it was a new one and widely different from Buckingham's.

In the first place Fielding abandoned those hampering inter-
ruptions of author, friends, and critics, common to all rehearsal
plays. *Tom Thumb* is a whole.

Second, although derived in one sense from *The Rehearsal*,
Tom Thumb (like *The What D'ye Call It*) took its principal inspiration, not from Buckingham's work, but from the tradition
of burlesque poetry. It was an adaptation for the stage of the
characteristic joke of *Le Lutrin*, *The Rape of the Lock*, *The Dunciad*,
and *Memoirs of P.P., Clerk of this Parish*.[2] The burlesque was
founded not so much in the parodies as in the general absurdity
of applying a tragic treatment to a theme as trivial as a nursery

---

[1] The 1730 *Tom Thumb* and the 1731 expansion, *The Tragedy of Tragedies*,
have been published together with useful prefaces, notes, and appendices,
by James T. Hillhouse (1918).
[2] The Scriblerus burlesque of Burnet's *History of My Own Times*.

rhyme. Besides, Fielding was not truly a parodist. He was a magpie. *Tom Thumb* is a nest-full of souvenirs, an anthology of nonsense collected from over forty plays. For the purpose of the joke the lines hardly needed parodying: it was enough to quote them.

Tom Thumb was a general burlesque. No specific heresy was being hunted. No particular poet was being savaged. Fielding may be very attached to Lee, but he does not pillory him as a Bayes. He was out for a laugh, not for chastisement. "What can be so proper for Tragedy as a Set of big sounding Words, so contrived together as to convey no Meaning; which I shall one day or other prove to be the Sublime of *Longinus*." So he blandly remarks in the preface—and Lord Grizzle's address to Huncamunca remains a splendid example of his intention.

> Oh! *Huncamunca, Huncamunca*, oh
> Thy pouting Breasts, like Kettle-Drums of Brass,
> Beat everlasting loud Alarms of Joy;
> As bright as Brass they are, and oh, as hard;
> Oh *Huncamunca, Huncamunca!* Oh![1]

Fielding's favourite joke was certainly the simile. *Tom Thumb* is packed with them, finely turned studies in fatuity, greatly aided by not being harnessed to parody. The simile already quoted [2] from Huncamunca's speech at the end of Act 2 is the subtlest example of a wicked art. Another admirable piece of nonsense concludes Lord Grizzle's dying speech.

> But, ha! I feel Death rumbling in my Brains,
> Some kinder Spright knocks softly at my Soul.
> And gently whispers it to haste away:
> I come, I come, most willingly I come.
> So; when some City Wife, for Country Air,
> To *Hampstead*, or to *Highgate* does repair;
> Her, to make haste, her Husband does implore,
> And cries, My Dear, *the Coach is at the Door.*
> With equal Wish, desirous to be gone,
> She gets into the Coach, and then she cries—Drive on!

---

[1] The allusion is to James Thompson's foolish line

> Oh! *Sophonisba! Sophonisba*, oh!

in *The Tragedy of Sophonisba* (1730).

[2] See p. 35.

This beautiful instance of "the Profound of *Scriblerus*" was suggested by a single line from Dryden's *The Conquest of Granada*—

> My Soul is packing up, and just on wing.

The element of parody exists therefore, but the passage remains an original creation, a means of laughter greatly superior to Buckingham's joke, which had made its point chiefly by the substitution of "boar and sow" for "turtles"—which was an easily won laugh.

Fielding's gusto for similes was unquenchable. In Act III Scene 2 the Ghost says "So have I seen" eight times in eight successive lines, and a footnote remarks *"A String of Similies* (says one) *proper to be hung up in the Cabinet of a Prince."* The King replies—

> D——n all thou'st seen!—Dost thou, beneath the Shape
> Of Gaffer *Thumb*, come hither to abuse me
> With Similies to keep me on the Rack?
> Hence—or by all the Torments of thy Hell,
> I'll run thee thro' the Body, tho' thou'st none.

It is this blank verse which marks another important difference between *Tom Thumb* and *The Rehearsal*. *The Rehearsal* had contained blank verse and couplets, but the main joke of composition had lain in the couplets. There were couplets in *Tom Thumb*—that joke was far too good to forget—but this time the main joke lay in the blank verse.

It had been Buckingham's pleasure to create lines of supreme feebleness.

> CORDELIO: His Highness Sirs, commanded me to tell you,
>   That the fair person whom you both do know,
>   Despairing of forgiveness for her fault,
>   In a deep sorrow, twice she did attempt
>   Upon her precious life; but, by the care
>   Of standers-by, prevented was.

It is an entertaining joke in moderation. But Fielding had a better one in a verse that was throbbing with life.

> GLUMDALCA: Left, scorn'd, and loath'd for such a Chit as this;
>   I feel the Storm that's rising in my Mind,
>   Tempests, and Whirlwinds rise, and rowl and roar.

I'm all within a Hurricane, as if
The World's four Winds were pent within my Carcass.
Confusion, Horror, Murder, Guts and Death.

'Guts' was an inspiration. Only by such a word could Fielding
have burlesqued a thing already so inflated as a tragedy oath.
An agreeable example of the real thing is, "Hell! Scalding
Lead! and Sulphures!" from Banks' *The Innocent Usurper*, and,
in *Oedipus*, Lee has

Night, Horrour, Death, Confusion, Hell and Furies!

No doubt a good actor could make either of these oaths
impressive: but no actor on earth could get away with Glumdalca's line.

The heroic oath was not one of Buckingham's jokes. *The
Rehearsal* goes no further than 'O ye Gods!' And 'there's a smart
expression of a passion", says Bayes, " . . . that's one of my bold
strokes a gad." The most flamboyant of the heroic dramas were
later than *The Rehearsal*, and the great burlesque tradition of
strong language finds its first vigorous expression here in *Tom
Thumb*. An unacted and anonymous play of 1723, *Love and
Friendship*, has

Cream! Custards! Cheesecakes! Apples! Ha! Ha—Oh!

                                                    [*dies.*

but that is a raving, like Kitty's couplet in *The What D'ye
Call It*: it is not a burlesque of bombast. This was the beginning.
Sheridan made no use of the joke, but almost exactly a hundred
years after *Tom Thumb* Planché was still writing "Gunpowder
and perdition!" and

Guns, trumpets, blunderbusses, drums and thunder!

suitable oaths for Mars in *The Paphian Bower* (1832). From
Planché the joke descended to the wicked characters of Victorian burlesque, and it is still to be heard at Christmas time
in the brimstone expletives of the pantomime demon. Thus the
language once dignified by the hero is at length relegated to the
other side.

Lastly Fielding distinguished his work by the addition of a
learned preface and copious notes, worthily derived from the

original Scriblerus, and burlesquing the critical manner of
Bentley and John Dennis.

> Petition me no Petitions, Sir, today;
> Let other Hours be set apart for Business.
> Today it is our Pleasure to be drunk,
> And this our Queen shall be as drunk as We.

Here is Fielding's note on the word 'drunk'—

An Expression vastly beneath the Dignity of Tragedy, says
Mr. D——s, yet we find the word he cavils at in the Mouth of
Mithridates less properly used and applied to a more terrible Idea.

> *I would be drunk with Death.* Mithrid.

The Author of the New *Sophonisba* taketh hold of this Monosyllable
and uses it pretty much to the same purpose.

> *The* Carthaginian *Sword with* Roman *Blood*
> *Was drunk.*

I would ask Mr. D——s which gives him the best Idea, a drunken
King or a drunken Sword?
Mr. *Tate* dresses up King *Arthur's* Resolution in Heroicks,

> *Merry, my Lord, o'th' Captain's Humour right,*
> *I am resolv'd to be dead drunk to Night.*

Lee also uses the charming Word:

> *Love's the Drunkenness of the Mind.* Gloriana.

There has been no parody at all; but the magpie's collection is
enriched by four treasures.

Tom Thumb takes an equal place with *The Rehearsal* in the
history of English stage burlesque. Fielding derived a great deal
from others—the couplet, the simile, the bluster, and the
slaughter from Buckingham, the bland nonsense from Swift
and Pope, the ghost and the discipline from Gay: but it was he
who brought these arts to perfection in the theatre, he who
created the most fatuous simile, he who provided the most
generous carnage and the most splendid ghost.[1] And it was he

---

[1] Fielding had an evident gusto for ghosts. There are four in *Pasquin* (see
pp. 32 and 61-2). He wrote of himself in *The Champion*, November 27,
1739, as "An Author who dealt so much in ghosts that he is said to have
spoiled the Haymarket stage by cutting it all into trap-doors." Ghosts were
certainly immensely popular. On April 20, 1711, Addison had written in

who introduced as a totally new joke a blank verse which had its own high standard of magnificence.

The Tragedy of Tragedies, in its original form, was acted in the London theatres up to 1755. In the provinces it was billed for many years after that date—which accounts for the publication of Miss Rose's portrait in the part of Tom Thumb in 1770.

In 1733 a version in one act with music by Arne was produced at the Haymarket as *The Opera of Operas*. Later in the same year a rival adaptation in three acts with music by John Frederick Lampe, was put on at Drury Lane. Not many performances are noted in Allardyce Nicoll's list, but Chetwood, in *A General History of the Stage* (1749), says it was "perform'd often". It was revived at Drury Lane in 1775, and, in 1780, Kane O'Hara produced his famous burletta of *Tom Thumb* at Covent Garden. This had a longer life than Fielding's original work, and remained in the repertoire long enough to influence Planché and the Victorians.[1]

The part of Tom Thumb was normally played by a child actor—not infrequently by an infant of only five years old. Perhaps the urchins of the 18th century theatre were built from more attractive material than the little gentlefolk of the modern acting school.

Fielding's next burlesque, *The Covent Garden Tragedy* (Drury Lane, 1732), has promoted an entertaining divergence of opinion between two modern critics. Allardyce Nicoll,[2] who finds the work "somewhat coarse reading", considers the travesty "at once vulgar and inartistic". W. E. Henley [3] admits

---

The Spectator, "There is nothing which delights and terrifies our *English* Theatre so much as a Ghost, especially when he appears in a bloody Shirt. A Spectre has very often saved a Play, though he has done nothing but Stalked across the Stage, or rose through a Cleft of it, and sunk again without speaking one word."

[1] It was a song from the O'Hara version of *Tom Thumb* that Jingle quoted at the White Hart Inn as he went out to obtain the licence for his marriage to Miss Wardle.

> In hurry, post-haste for a licence,
> In hurry, ding dong I come back.
>   (*The Pickwick Papers*, Chapter X.)

[2] *A History of Early Eighteenth Century Drama* (1923).
[3] *The Complete Works of Henry Fielding* (1903).

the rudeness but not the lack of art. "*The Covent Garden Tragedy*", says he, "is altogether too naughty and too riotous to be included in any list of Masterpieces of the English Drama. . . . Yet a masterpiece it is."

"Vulgar and inartistic", or "a masterpiece?" Which?

In *The Covent Garden Tragedy* Fielding was burlesquing not all the tragedies of the past sixty years, but a single one of them —*The Distrest Mother* (1712) by Ambrose Phillips derived from Racine. The "somewhat coarse reading" may be granted at once. *The Distrest Mother*, being a tragedy of love, was easily mocked in a play whose setting was the establishment of Mother Punchbowl, a London bawd. Pyrrhus is Lovegirlo, a visitor at Mother Punchbowl's establishment. Andromache and Hermione are Kissinda and Stormandra, members of Mother Punchbowl's sorority. Captain Bilkum is Orestes.

There must be many topical hits in every burlesque, which are quite lost to succeeding generations. A letter of Horace Walpole's reveals the unexpected intelligence that Bilkum refers to a man who was later tragically famous in America as General Braddock. According to Walpole, Braddock was kept by a Mrs. Upton, whom he used as infamously as Bilkum uses Stormandra at the beginning of the play.

Fielding made no attempt to parody particular passages in *The Distrest Mother*. He was writing a general burlesque of the whole story. In particular he was burlesquing Ambrose Phillips's portentous style—of which Andromache's final speech may serve as an opulent example.

> Oh Cephisa!
> A springing joy, mix't with a soft concern,
> A pleasure which no language can express,
> An ecstasy that mothers only feel,
> Plays round my heart, and brightens up my sorrow,
> Like gleams of sunshine ina lowering sky.
> Though plung'd in ills, and exercis'd in care,
> Yet never let the noble mind despair:
> When press'd by dangers, and beset with foes
> The gods their timely succour interpose;
> And when our virtue sinks, o'erwhelm'd with grief,
> By unforeseen expedients, bring relief.

To this sort of stuff Fielding opposed a rival story exquisitely unbecoming to the dignity of blank verse. Hear Gallono addressing his friend Lovegirlo:

> And wilt thou leave us for a woman thus?
> Art thou Lovegirlo? Tell me, art thou he
> Whom I have seen the saffron-coloured morn
> With rosy fingers beckon home in vain?
> Thou whom none oftner pull'd the pendent bell,
> None oftner cried, 'another bottle bring';
> And canst thou leave us for a worthless woman?

And later, when Gallono makes this splendid remonstrance to Mother Punchbowl :

> Give me my friend, thou most accursed bawd;
> Restore him to me drunken as he was
> Ere thy vile arts seduc'd him from the glass.

Several fine similies are put in the unsuitable mouth of Bilkum, and there are raving speeches, in the correct tragedy manner, for Bilkum, Mother Punchbowl, Gallono, and Kissinda.

> O! give me way; come, all you furies, come
> Lodge in th' unfurnished chambers of my heart:
> My heart, which never shall be let again
> To any guest but endless misery,
> Never shall have a bill upon it more.

Which, apart from its wit, is better sense than the silly statement of Andromache's at which it glances:

> While I live, my tears
> Will never cease; for I was born to grieve.

The Covent Garden Tragedy was an essay—and at length—in the humours of 18th century blank verse. It had not been done before and it antedated *The Critic* by nearly fifty years. It was a difficult undertaking admirably performed. Vulgar it certainly is: but it is also a masterpiece of sustained burlesque.

In *Pasquin*, performed at the Haymarket in 1736, Fielding returned to the rehearsal play, and in doing so reverted to a more satirical kind of writing: indeed it is described in the title as "a dramatic satire". A comedy and a tragedy are in rehearsal. The comedy is good irony on political bribery: the tragedy describes the rebellion of Firebrand, (the priest of the Sun), Law, and Physick, against the rule of Queen Common-Sense. Queen Ignorance, with their connivance, invades Queen Common-Sense's dominions, attended by "Singers, Fiddlers, Rope-Dancers, Tumblers, etc." Common-Sense is defeated, and slain by the treacherous Firebrand. But Ignorance does not triumph. She is scared from the country she has won by the arrival of Common-Sense's ghost.

All this gives a wide opportunity for satirical cracks at priests, lawyers, doctors, Harlequin, and opera. But purposeful laughter is not the same thing as laughing for fun, and *Pasquin* is not a carefree burlesque like *Tom Thumb* or *The Covent Garden Tragedy*. The interesting thing about it is that, in spite of the satire, Fielding has nevertheless contrived to make it a remarkable repository of the best jokes of the burlesque tradition. *Pasquin* is a sort of dramatic stock-taking of the burlesque treasury.

First comes an echo of Buckingham's joke when the Physician opens his conversation with the Usher with the words, "Sir, to conclude"—and Bayes explains that "they had been talking of this a pretty while without." [1]

MISS: Ha! and can you be so generous to forgive all my ill
          usage of you?
FUSTIAN: What ill usage, Mr. Trapwit! For if I mistake not, this
          is the first time these lovers spoke to one another.
TRAPWIT: What ill usage, Sir? a great deal, Sir.
FUSTIAN: When, Sir? Where, Sir?
TRAPWIT: Why, behind the scenes, Sir. What—would you have
          everything brought upon the stage?

So Fielding keeps a good joke warm for the opening lines of Puff's play forty-three years later—"True, gallant Raleigh." [2]
There are four ghosts, (Gay and Duffett had both gone in for numbers) and one of them has the splendid joke, already quoted,[3] of being called hence before he has time to deliver his message—which is a twist of that joke in *The Rehearsal* where Amaryllis would have had a fine speech "but that they hinder'd her". The two-man army joke also goes back to *The Rehearsal*.

[1] See pp. 31–2.   [2] See p. 32.   [3] See p. 32.

The joke of the thunder and lightning failing to come off is an inversion of Duffett's earlier joke when they come off all too well.[1] And the sort of stage-managerial joke which Buckingham would have enjoyed is played in the singularly fatuous battle scene.

Then there is the discipline and gravity, a burlesque accomplishment fostered by the Scriblerus group and in the theatre carried to perfection by Fielding: an agreeable moment when the Ghost of Common-Sense comes on a scene too early—"'S death, Madam, I tell you, you are no ghost, you are not kill'd": and finally, the blank verse, Fielding's own speciality, and as good as ever.

In *The Author's Farce* and *Pasquin* Harlequin had been brought in as one character among several lined up for punishment. In *Tumble-Down Dick* (1736) "invented by the ingenious Monsieur Sans Esprit. The Musick composed by the harmonious Signior Warblerini. And the scenes painted by the prodigious Mynheer Van Bottom-Flat", Fielding set out to do something much more important—a complete burlesque of a particular pantomime production at Drury Lane. For the student of Pantomime *Tumble-Down Dick* is engrossing, both for the sake of the fully described business, and for the occasional interpolated remarks, such as: "You know, Sir, or may know, that Aristotle, in his book concerning entertainments, has laid it down as a principal rule, that Harlequin is always to escape."

For the student of burlesque the work is interesting for a number of hits at the dance, scenery, effects, and stage-management. It is obvious that at the time the piece must have been highly entertaining.

Two other rehearsal plays of 1737, *The Historical Register for the year 1736* and *Eurydice Hiss'd* are only important in the history of burlesque for two curious particulars. In *The Historical Register*, when the rehearsal play begins, five politicians are discovered, sitting at a table. "Here's a mistake in the print, Mr. Medley," says Sourwit. "I observe the second politician is the first person who speaks". "Sir," answers Medley, "my first and greatest politician never speaks at all, he is a very deep man. . . ." The second curiosity is to be found at the end

[1] See pp. 39–40.

of *Eurydice Hiss'd* in a whirling speech by Pillage, the author, which finishes thus:

> Now my brain's on fire!
> My staggering senses dance—and I am—
> HONESTUS: Drunk.
> That word he should have said, that ends the verse.

Here, tucked away in two unimportant pieces are the obvious originals of two of Sheridan's most famous jokes—his superb presentation of Burleigh in the act of cogitation, and Whiskerandos's dying line—

> And Whiskerandos quits this bustling scene
> For all eter-
> BEEFEATER: -nity—he would have added, but stern death
> Cut short his being, and the noun at once.[1]

There would soon be an end to laughter if the humorists were forbidden to build upon each other's jokes. The best of them improve and develop them, turn them about, and adapt them to new situations. Sheridan here makes the split sentence joke twice as funny by making Puff ask the actors to do the death scene again. A less gifted author can only copy the last man. W. B. Rhodes in *Bombastes Furioso* (1810) has

> Oh! Oh! My Bom-
> BOMBASTES: bastes he would have said.
> But 'ere the word was out his breath was fled.

The burlesque humour of Henry Fielding sometimes enlivened even the advertisements. A lot of fun was got out of the enormously successful *Pasquin*. In March and early April 1736 notices of benefits for Trapwit and Fustian (authors of the comedy and tragedy rehearsed in *Pasquin*) were exhibited at length in *The London Daily Post*. In Trapwit's announcement the poet begs that the spectators "take no Notice of the Tragedy but attend very closely to the Comedy, there being several fresh Jokes new cloath'd at second Hand, for the Use of that Night"; while Fustian "desires the Audience (notwithstanding

---

[1] Professor G. H. Nettleton misses this derivation from *Eurydice Hiss'd* in his preface on the sources of *The Critic* in *The Major Dramas of Richard Brinsley Sheridan* (1906).

his Brother Trapwit's unfair Advertisement to the contrary) to take particular Notice of the Tragedy, there being several New and very deep Things to be spoke by the Ghost of Tragedy, if the Cock does not crow him away too soon". Fustian also promises that "Particular Care will be taken to get the Thunder and Lightning in Order".

These over-flows of Fielding's humour are also burlesques of the actor's benefit advertisement. Fustian's announcement begins as follows:—

For the Benefit of POET FUSTIAN
At the particular Desire of all the Friends
of COMMON SENSE
By the Great Mogul's *company of* English *Comedians*
Newly Imported

And both notices end with a burlesque of the usual instructions about the sale of tickets. "N.B.", says Trapwit, "As there is little Hope of a great Demand of Tickets, or Places for that Evening, the Doors will be open'd by Six o'Clock in the Morning, and constant Attendance the whole Day given, for fear any Application should be made for either."

At the end of the same month, April, 1736, the advertisements for *Tumble-Down Dick* included in the *Dramatis Personae*, "Constables, Watchmen, Fidlers, Lanthorns, Suns, Moons, Stars, Devils, Salamanca Doctors, Whores, &c. &c. &c."— which was all part of Fielding's burlesque of pantomime in general, and *The Fall of Phaeton*, at Drury Lane, in particular.

Benefit notices in May refer to "the Country Interest" (i.e. the Opposition)—a reminder that all Fielding's burlesques were also satires aimed at the heart of Robert Walpole.

Digression as it must be, it would be wrong to leave Henry Fielding without recording his almost certain authorship of *An Apology for The Life of Mrs. Shamela Andrews* (1741)—a parody burlesque of Richardson's *Pamela*, and the earliest burlesque of the modern novel. Written with a straight face and with no facetious parentheses to underline and spoil a joke, *Shamela* is one of the best burlesques ever written. It is an extremely improper book, but it would be wholly mistaken to suppose that Fielding was writing nothing but a bawdy squib.

He had a prophylactic purpose as strong as Buckingham had when he attacked heroic tragedy. Fielding was repelled by the high moral tone in *Pamela*, and in this shameful story, in which Shamela is shown to be a designing minx and the mistress of a parson, he makes a just reply to Richardson's mawkishness.[1] The book is written in the form of letters between Shamela and her mother, commonly beginning with a detailed description of man-chasing, and ending with remarks like "I have enclosed for you one of Mr. Whitefield's sermons". The whole thing is admirably done and irresistibly funny; but unfortunately it does not lend itself to discreet quotation.

The Dedication is an equally agreeable skit on a dedication to Lord Hervey in a Life of Cicero by Dr. Middleton.[2]

In 1742 Fielding published another book which proposed at the outset to describe the trials and temptations of Pamela's brother, Joseph. As a burlesque it did not get very far, for, in describing Joseph's encounters with Lady Booby and Mrs. Slipslop, Fielding discovered his genius for character creation, and, in falling upon Parson Adams, he forgot about *Pamela* and began to write what he afterwards claimed as "a comic epic poem in prose", "written in imitation of the manner of Cervantes". He was, in fact, shifting the structure of the English novel from the sands of romantic anecdote to the firm ground of ironic comedy.

HENRY CAREY

THE burlesques of Henry Carey overlapped with Fielding's. *Chrononhotonthologos* (by Benjamin Bounce Esqr.) was produced in 1734, *The Dragon of Wantley* in 1737 and *Margery* (also known as *The Dragoness*) in 1738.

Carey is important because of his delight in pure extravagance, because he maintained the idea of writing complete pieces, and because his work is not punitive. He savaged

---

[1] In spite of its phenomenal success *Pamela* was widely reprobated by others beside Fielding. See Archibald Bolling Shepperson's *The Novel In Motley* (1936) Chapter 2.

[2] *Shamela* was reprinted in 1926, edited by R. Brimley Johnson. Another edition was published in 1930 with an introduction by Brian W. Downs.

Ambrose Phillips [1] in "Namby-Pamby"—but in his theatrical
work he seems to have reached that best stage of burlesque,
where the artist can fairly be grateful to bombast, or the
Italian opera, for the joyful opportunities which his victims
afford him.

The purpose of *Chrononhotonthologos* is plainly described in
the Prologue.

> *To Night our Comic* MUSE *the Buskin wears,*
> *And gives herself no small Romantic Airs;*
> Struts in Heroics, and in pompous Verse
> Does the minutest Incidents rehearse;
> In Ridicule's strict Retrospect displays
> The Poetasters of these modern Days;
> Who with big bellowing Bombast rend our Ears,
> Which, stript of Sound, quite void of Sense appears;
> Or else their Fiddle-Faddle Numbers flow
> Serenely dull, elaborately low. . . .

The play starts off with lines which are still familiar to many.

> [*Enter* RIGDUM-FUNNIDOS *and* ALDIBORONTIPHOSCOPHORNIO
> RIG.-FUN.: Aldiborontiphoscophornio!
> Where left you Chrononhotonthologos?
> ALDI.:   Fatigu'd with the tremendous Toils of War,
> Within his Tent, on downy Couch succumbent,
> Himself he unfatigues with gentle Slumbers.

It is remarkable that, so soon after *Tom Thumb*, another man
could play the same joke and yet play it so differently. Carey's
joke is concerned with the bombastic manner in general, not
with the minute discovery of particular follies. It is not better
than Fielding's, but it adds something to it.

> ALDI.: But, lo! the King his Footsteps this Way bending
> His cogitative Faculties immers'd
> In Cogibundity of Cogitation:
> Let Silence close our Folding Doors of Speech,
> 'Till apt Attention tell our Heart the Purport
> Of this profound Profundity of Thought.

Then there is the Queen, drivelling away in the fiddle-
faddle technique, with a fine example of "sinking" at the end.

[1] See p. 9.

QUEEN: Day's Curtains drawn, the Morn begins to rise,
And waking Nature rubs her sleepy Eyes:
And pretty little fleecy bleating Flocks
In Baas harmonious warble thro' the Rocks:
Night gathers up her Shades in sable Shrouds,
And whisp'ring Oziers tattle to the Clouds.
What think you, Ladies, if an hour we kill
At Basset, Ombre, Picquet, or Quadrille?

The plot of this "Most Tragical Tragedy that was ever Tragedized by any Company of Tragedians" is an extremely sketchy affair, and the main burlesque of bombastic drama is twice interrupted, first by "a grand Pantomime Entertainment", and later by an elegant episode of opera. Carey was hitting out all round, and the result was inevitably disjointed.

The burlesque of the pantomime is, of course, lost: the joke would have been entirely a visual one. During its performance the Captain of the Guard rushes in and informs Chrononhotonthologos that

Th' Antipodean Pow'rs, from Realms below,
Have burst the solid Entrails of the Earth;
Gushing such Catracts of Forces forth,
This world is too incopious to contain 'em.

At Chrononhotonthologos's mighty glance, however, the Antipodeans flee "as fast as their Hands could carry 'em", leaving their king behind, a prisoner. Queen Fadladinida falls in love with him (a common event in contemporary tragedy), and visiting the topsy-turvy king in prison, she invokes the aid of Venus and Cupid. Venus descends in a chariot and sings. Then Cupid descends and sings a song in the ballad style of musical burlesque, ending with these lines.

You shall be a Widow before it is Night,
Gilly Flow'r, Gentle Rosemary.
No longer a Maiden so fair and so bright
As the Dew that flies over the Mulberry Tree.
Two jolly young Husbands your Person shall share
Gilly Flow'r etc.
And twenty fine babies all lovely and fair
As the Dew etc.

QUEEN: O thanks, Mr. Cupid! for this your good News
        Gilly Flow'r etc.
  What Woman alive would such Favours refuse?
        While the Dew etc.
    VENUS *and* CUPID *re-ascend; the Queen goes off, and the*
    King of the Antipodes follows, walking on his hands.

The King of the Antipodes has nothing to say and he only
appears in that one scene; but in an age when acrobatic performance was infinitely more skilful than it is today, the part
may well have been more amusing than it appears on paper.

The prison scene had been used by Gay in *The Beggar's
Opera*, and was mentioned in The Prologue to that work as one
"which the Ladies always reckon charmingly pathetick".
Many years later Frere and Canning were to revive it in their
burlesque of that German drama which specialized in Gothic
vaults and horrid scenes of incarceration.[1] In the 20th century
Max Beerbohm has preserved the joke in *Savonarola Brown*.

The rest of the play is concerned with the quarrel between
Chrononhotonthologos and General Bombardinian. The
General kills his sovereign in a fit of drunken anger, and then
raves in lines which so pleased Sir Walter Scott [2] that he set
them at the head of the first chapter of *The Antiquary*.

            Ha! What have I done?
   Go, call a Coach, and let a Coach be call'd;
   And let the Man that calls it be the Caller;
   And in his Calling, let him nothing call,
   But Coach! Coach! Coach! Oh! for a Coach, ye Gods!
                       [Exit raving.

After which, in fulfilment of Cupid's prophecy, the Queen
calmly arranges to marry both Rigdum-Funnidos and Aldiborontiphoscophornio—a burlesque joke, borrowed from Tom
Thumb, which was to find a target many years later in Goethe's
outrageous double arrangement at the end of *Stella*.[3]

Chrononhotonthologos is the most muddled of all the burlesques.
Even allowing for deliberate malice in the mixing, the ingredients were too many for one brief work. Carey's next burlesque

---

[1] See p. 84.
[2] Scott used to call the printers, James and John Ballantyne, Rigdum-
Funnidos and Aldiborontiphoscophornio.
[3] See pp. 81-6.

was not so funny, but it was better disciplined and infinitely more successful.

The Dragon of Wantley was produced at Covent Garden eight months after Handel's *Justin* had failed at the same theatre—with "no lack of bears, fantastic animals, and dragons vomiting fire".[1] In his *Memoirs* Lord Hervey describes George II talking about *The Dragon of Wantley* to the company in the Drawing Room, and adds, on his own account, "This was a new silly farce which everybody at this time went to see." Silly or not, it is certain that everybody went to see it. *The Dragon of Wantley* was played sixty-seven times in its first season—five performances above the more famous run of The Beggar's Opera nine years earlier.[2]

It is worth noting that, in 1732, Carey and the composer, John Frederick Lampe, had attempted a serious opera "after the Italian manner". But *Amelia* only scored twelve performances—a hard fact which doubtless persuaded the collaborators to consider the Italian manner from another angle. *Teraminta*, another opera written by Carey in 1732, was only performed three times.

Gay had burlesqued the opera obliquely by the ironical substitution of English folk tunes for the elaborate arias of Italy. Carey (Carini for the purpose of this work) burlesqued the opera directly. "Many joyous hours have we shared during its Composition", he writes in his dedication to Lampe—

chopping and changing, lopping, eking out, and coining of Words, Syllables, and Jingle, to display in *English* the Beauty of Nonsense, so prevailing in *Italian Operas*.

This Pleasure has been since transmitted to the gay, the goodnatur'd, and jocular Part of Mankind, who have tasted the Joke and enjoy'd the Laugh; while the Morose, the Supercilious, and Assinine have been fairly taken in, so far as to be downright angry;

---

[1] Victor Schoelcher *Life of Handel* (1857) p. 185.

[2] Pope wrote in a note to *The Dunciad* that *The Beggar's Opera* had been performed "Sixty-three days without intermission". He was wrong in both his facts. The number was sixty-two, and the run was not continuous. See *The Beggar's Opera, its Content, History and Influence* by W. E. Schultz. Fielding's *Pasquin*, in its one year of existence, also had a longer run than *The Beggar's Opera* in its first season but at a smaller theatre.

they say 'tis low, very low; now (begging their Worships Pardon)
I affirm it to be sublime, very sublime—

> It is a Burlesque Opera:
> And Burlesque cannot be too low.

Lowness (figuratively speaking) is the Sublimity of Burlesque:
If so, *this Opera* is, consequently, the tip-top Sublime of its kind.

Carey's mention of "the gay, the good-natur'd, and jocular
Part of Mankind" is reminiscent of Davenant's "Men of no
malice who will pay for laughter",[1] and is evidence of the
absence from this work of any true bitterness.

In a burlesque of opera the music must necessarily make at
least half the joke. This is lost in the printed book, but we know
from the *Biographia Dramatica* that "the songs, though ludicrous
in the highest degree, were set perfectly in the Italian taste".
It is not difficult to guess the kind of music he made for Carey's
final chorus.

> *Sing, Sing, and rorio,*
> *An* Oratorio
> *To gallant* Morio,
> *Of* Moore-Hall.
> *To* Margerenia
> *Of* Roth'ram—Greenia,
> *Beauty's bright Queenia,*
> *Bellow and bawl.*

Charles Dibdin wrote in his *History of the Stage* that *The
Dragon of Wantley* was "much more the right sort of burlesque
on Italian operas than the generality of pieces written upon
that principle". The composer of *The Opera of Operas*, *The
Dragon of Wantley*, and *The Comick Masque of Pyramus and
Thisbe* (for Lampe wrote a new version of Leveridge's skit in
1745) has earned an honourable place in the burlesque tradition.

Carey's burlesques were not constructed as carefully as Gay's
or Fielding's, but his efflorescent and polysyllabic humour long
remained a model, though no one else copied it with quite the
same abandonment to laughter. *Chrononhotonthologos* has perhaps
exercised a more lasting influence on English burlesque than

[1] See p. 29.

any other work in the canon. Sixty years after it was written people were laughing at an actor who played the Queen in the manner of Mrs. Siddons. It was in the bill at Drury Lane as late as 1815; it was an obvious ancestor of *Bombastes Furioso* (1810) and several minor works with such titles as *Rumfustian Innamorato* (1824) and *Leatherlungos the Great* (1872); it influenced the extravaganza writers, and even Bernard Shaw borrowed from it in *The Admirable Bashville*.

RICHARD BRINSLEY SHERIDAN

THE forty years between *Margery* (1738) and *The Critic* (1779) added nothing to the burlesque tradition in the theatre. Kitty Clive had a laugh at the opera and women writers, in *Bayes in Petticoats* (1750) and Garrick wrote yet another rehearsal play *A Peep behind the Curtain* (1767), burlesquing the burletta. More in the old tradition was *Distress Upon Distress* (1752) by George Alexander Stevens, which claimed to have "all the Similies, Rants, Groans, Sighs etc., entirely new"; and *Madrigal and Truletta* (1758) by Joseph Reed.[1] *The Tailors* (1767) is burlesque only because the subject is beneath the dignity of blank verse. None of these works discovered any fresh jokes or improved upon any old one: indeed *The Court of Alexander* (1770), also by Stevens, is hardly a burlesque at all. Here is a 'mad' song, and a simile, and the couplet proper to the occasion, but the effect is not more than farcical.[2]

Burlesque feeds upon follies—and it needed some new ones. Pantomime and opera were jokes long familiar and the basic joke of heroic tragedy was a centenarian. In 1773 Samuel Foote attacked a worthy folly in *Piety in Pattens*, a piece, which "consisted of the most trifling and common-place thoughts,

[1] In a reply to a critic the author pathetically remarks that the show might have been a success if better cast, "for that the Play was most inhumanly butcher'd in the representation none will deny; for if ever so compleat a Collection of *Theatrical Wretches* was, in any one Play, brought upon the Stage of a *Theatre Royal*, I will venture to renounce all Pretensions to Common-Sense".

[2] The principal interest in this piece is its general likeness to the classical extravaganzas of the 19th century Planché, rather than to the burlesque of Carey, Fielding or Buckingham.

wrapped up in a bundle of grand phrases and high-flown words; and had its full effect as a laughable burlesque on forced sentiment".[1] But *Piety in Pattens* was only a one-act play. It had no particular success and was never published. Six years later *The Critic* not only attacked all the follies of the contemporary stage at once, but revived and preserved within the compass of the work almost the whole canon of the burlesque tradition.

The debt of Sheridan to the earlier burlesque writers is large and unconcealed. Buckingham had made the fundamental jokes behind the opening conversation,[2] and the Beefeater's soliloquy.[3] Fielding had already burlesqued the discovery scene,[4] the split sentence,[5] the thinking actor,[6] and, in particular, blank verse. Duels and battles and effects had been burlesqued by Duffett, Buckingham, Fielding, and Carey. Sheridan helped himself deliberately to everything of value in the burlesque tradition—excepting only the ghost, the similes, the oaths and the rhymed couplets, for the exclusion of which there was an obvious reason.[7] These things belonged to the heroic play, and by Sheridan's day the heroic play was dead. The drama had grown romantic and sentimental. Classical subjects had given place to stories from English history. Shakespeare had been revived and refurbished, and historical spectacles, especially after the Stratford Jubilee of 1769, had become increasingly popular. It was a new sort of tragedy that Sheridan had to burlesque, and that he did it effectively is shown by a notice of the first edition of *The Critic*, in *The Critical Review* (November 1781): "Certain however it is, that since the exhibition of *The Critic*, tragedy, which a celebrated writer has declared to be one of the greatest exertions of the human mind, is fallen into contempt; it will be some time at least before she can recover the blow."

Unlike *The Rehearsal*, *The Critic* depends very little upon close parody, indeed Professor G. H. Nettleton only identifies one

---

[1] *Recollections of John O'Keefe* (1826). The manuscript of *Piety in Pattens* is in the Larpent Collection in the Henry F. Huntingdon Collection in California.

[2] See p. 31.   [3] See p. 32.   [4] See p. 52.
[5] See p. 63.   [6] See p. 62.

[7] There was of course no killing the rhymed couplet. They are back in *Bombastes Furioso* (1810) and were to be the medium for all the extravaganzas and pantomimes of the 19th century. In pantomime they survive to this day.

clear parallel in the whole work.[1] There are more than that. The opening scene of Hannah More's fatuous tragedy *Percy* (produced December 1777, a year and a half before *The Critic*) contains a brief example of that exchange of known facts which is the principal joke of the opening conversation in *The Critic*.

DOUGLAS: . . . Well then, the King of England—
EDRIC: Is expected
    From distant Palestine.
DOUGLAS: Forbid it Heaven!
    For with him comes——

which is very like and nearly as funny as the conversation of Sir Walter and Sir Christopher:[2]

SIR WALTER: . . . The famed Armada—by the Pope Baptized,
    With Purpose to invade these Realms—
SIR CHRISTOPHER: Is sailed.
    Our last advices so report.

Certainly Sheridan had his eye, too, on Richard Cumberland, whose singularly unhistorical tragedy *The Battle of Hastings* had been produced at Drury Lane in 1778.

In their new-found pre-occupation with Shakespeare and English History, certain dramatists had made themselves ludicrously eager to reproduce the precise phraseology of the 16th century. Cumberland's smooth blank verse is by no means ill written, but it is brimming over with half-remembered fragments of Shakespeare.

(*a*) Hors'd on the sightless winds . . .
(*b*) Why stand these guards like hounds upon the slip?
(*c*) There fled a mighty soul—Angels receive it
    And waft it to the mansions of the blest.
(*d*) Strike off his head! By him who made the heavens,
    Whose great primaeval interdiction cries
    Thro' all creation's round, thou shalt not kill,
    I do adjure you stop!
(*e*)   'Tis the cause,
    The cause . . .
(*f*) The grey-eyed morn.

It was this sort of thing that marked down Cumberland as Sir Fretful Plagiary, and this sort of thing that pointed the

[1] The recognition scene (see pp. 52–3) which certainly burlesques a scene in Home's *Douglas*.   [2] See p. 34.

great moment in Puff's play, when the Beefeater goes the whole distance and begins his soliloquy with the complete line from *Othello*:

Perdition catch my soul but I *do* love thee!

Cumberland's weakness for an echo had provided the burlesque tradition with a brand new joke—one which more than a century later, Max Beerbohm was to work with brilliant effect in *Savonarola Brown*.

Besides the obvious hit at Cumberland's (probably unconscious) plagiarisms, there is surely a link between Puff's "small sword logic" and the chopped dialogue of Edgar and Harold in Cumberland's play.

HAROLD: Then art thou lost—Oh yet preserve thy country!
EDGAR: My honour and my oath—
HAROLD: Thy life—
EDGAR: My love.
HAROLD: Die then! What hoa! my guards. Strike off his head.

The dialogue between Tilburina and the Governor glances askew at this passage, though Sheridan lifts the joke above the merits of parody by extending it into an exquisite and unlooked for absurdity.

TILBURINA: A Retreat in Spain!
GOVERNOR: Outlawry here!
TILBURINA: Your Daughter's Prayer!
GOVERNOR: Your Father's Oath!
TILBURINA: My Lover!
GOVERNOR: My Country!
TILBURINA: Tilburina!
GOVERNOR: England!
TILBURINA: A title!
GOVERNOR: Honour!
TILBURINA: A Pension!
GOVERNOR: Conscience!
TILBURINA: A Thousand Pounds!
GOVERNOR: Ha! thou hast touch'd me nearly.

There are these few probable instances of specific parody in *The Critic*. But in the main the work is certainly a general burlesque of contemporary tragedy, with a special affection, one may guess, for *The Battle of Hastings*—for Sheridan's finest thrust was against the period's bogus Elizabethan verse, in which none was a greater proficient than Richard Cumberland. *The Battle of Hastings* is conducted in a spate of garrulity. Even a common command becomes "Herald, provoke the bugle: spread the joy", and Edwina indicates her feminine distaste for battle in a speech which gathers wind as it rolls towards its ultimate bathos.

> Power supreme!
> Whose word can bid the gathering clouds disperse,
> Smooth the vext bosom of the furrow'd sea,
> And chain the stubborn and contentious winds,
> When they unseat the everlasting rocks
> And cast them to the sky, wilt thou permit
> Thy creature man thus to deface thy works?
> Or is he stronger and in less controul
> Than these fierce elements?

The Battle of Hastings is full of this sort of writing. Sheridan did not parody it: he burlesqued it in general in the splendid encounter between Leicester, Hatton, Raleigh, and the Governor.

LEICESTER: How's this, my friends! is 't thus your new-fledg'd zeal
> And plumed valour moulds in roosted sloth? . . .
> Can the quick current of a Patriot Heart
> Thus stagnate in a cold and weedy converse,
> Or freeze in Tideless Inactivity?
> No rather let the Fountain of your Valour
> Spring through each stream of enterprise,
> Each petty channel of conducive Daring,
> Till the full torrent of your foaming Wrath
> O'erwhelm the Flats of sunk Hostility.

SIR WALTER: No more! The freshening Breath of thy Rebuke
> Hath fill'd the swelling canvas of our Souls
> And thus, tho' fate should cut the cable of
>   [*All take hands.*
> Our topmost hopes—in Friendship's closing line
> We'll grapple with despair, and if we fall
> We'll fall in glory's Wake.

This is creative burlesque, infinitely superior to the giggle of precise parody. Fielding had developed the joke in *The Covent Garden Tragedy*. Sheridan brought it to this grave perfection. In the 20th century Max Beerbohm turned it about, matching the splendour of Sheridan's blank verse with the unparalleled flatness of Ladbroke Brown's.

Along with the portentous verse came certain other jokes founded in the contemporary drama. Whiskerandos, the romantic hero, and Tilburina, the sentimental heroine, were flowers fresh gathered from the garden of contemporary nonsense—for the splendid women of the heroic drama had given place to more gentle spirits, and there is nothing of Huncamunca's militant mind in the floral conceits of Tilburina.

> Now Flowers unfold their Beauties to the Sun,
> And blushing kiss the Beam he sends to wake them—
> The strip'd Carnation, and the guarded Rose,
> The vulgar Wall Flower, and smart Gilly flower,
> The Polyanthus mean—the dapper Daisy,
> Sweet William, and sweet marjorum—and all
> The Tribe of single and of double Pinks!
> Now too the feather'd Warblers tune their Notes
> Around, and charm the listening Grove. The lark!
> The Linnet, Chaffinch, Bullfinch, Goldfinch, Greenfinch!
> —But O to me no joy can they afford
> Nor Rose, nor Wallflower, nor smart Gillyflow'r,
> Nor Polyanthus mean, nor dapper Daisy,
> Nor William sweet, nor marjorum—nor Lark,
> Linnet, nor all the finches of the grove!

In 1778 France and Spain had allied themselves with the American colonists, and in August 1779 the combined French and Spanish fleets had lain off Plymouth, provoking for a short while considerable consternation. *The Critic* was produced on October 30, 1779, and Puff's play *The Spanish Armada*, with its grand finale—"*Flourish of drums . . . trumpets . . . cannon &c. &c. Scene changes to the sea—the fleets engage—the musick plays 'Britons strike home' . . . Spanish fleet destroyed by fire-ships &c. . . . English fleet advances . . . musick plays 'Rule Britannia'*"—bore a topical significance which is now forgotten. Acceptable as all that must have been, it marks equally a beginning of that burlesque patriotic joke, to which—to the confusion and astonishment of their neighbours—the English have so long been addicted. Increasingly throughout the century plays had been garnished with patriotic sentiments. The more that England fought in distant continents, the more did heroes of the stage pledge themselves to the defence of their country. "England and Edwina!" murmurs the gallant Edgar in *The Battle of Hastings* while Matilda urges on the Saxon armies with—

> Go, ye brave English; go, as ye are wont,
> To glorious conquest: Oh remember, friends,
> Ye strike for us, for freedom, for your country.

Battles had often been burlesqued before—but usually by making them fatuous. Sheridan made the joke the other way round, burlesquing not with a minimum but with an excess of patriotic splendour. "The scene of the battle with the Armada", writes the critic of *The London Chronicle*, was "executed in the most masterly manner". According to *The Public Advertiser* it was "miraculous".

Earlier in the play the beefeater had resolved an impasse by ordering everyone to drop their weapons "in the Queen's name" (which they instantly do). This magnificent surrender of reason to the call of loyalty is another aspect of the patriotic joke.

One hundred and one years later Gilbert revived it in *The Pirates of Penzance* when the Police subdue the Pirate band with

> We charge you yield, in Queen Victoria's name!

Seven years later he broadened the joke in *Ruddigore*.

RICHARD: Hold—we are prepared for this (*producing a Union Jack*). Here is a flag that none dare defy (*all kneel*), and while this glorious rag floats over Rose Maybud's head, the man does not live who would dare to lay unlicensed hand upon her!

Since Gilbert the joke has been seen again and again in burlesques, where the flag, accompanied by "Home Sweet Home", may always be guaranteed to reduce chaos to order and rebellion to obedience.

The sea battle was not the end of *The Spanish Armada*. The finale of the finale was a "procession of all the English rivers and their tributaries with their emblems etc.", beginning with Handel's Water music, and ending with a chorus to the march in *Judas Maccabaeus*. The rivers, so Puff had explained, were to compliment Britannia with a fête in honour of the victory—and if this may be taken literally we may suppose that it marks the first appearance in burlesque of that popular national figure, whose shield, helmet, and trident have given so much pleasure to so many thousands of theatre-goers.

Processions were one of the dearest vanities of the Georgian Theatre. Garrick's Shakespeare Jubilee had been a tremendous display; there was a famous funeral procession in *Romeo and Juliet*; and *Henry VIII* was chiefly popular for the coronation procession of Anne Boleyn. In *The Morning Chronicle*, April 30, 1779, there is an advertisement of a play called *Gallic Gratitude: or The Frenchman in India*. This Covent Garden production contained "an Indian Procession and a Prologue by Mrs. Jackson in the character of BRITANNIA". It is impossible to spot all the probable allusions in *The Critic*, but one certainly can not ignore *Gallic Gratitude* : it may well have been the last straw.

Our own times have seen a revival both of the serious procession and of its burlesque.

In the 1930's there were many touring revues with titles like *One Night in Paris* and *Sous le Rideau* (such a title being kindly translated on poster and programme for the benefit of the uneducated). These shows regularly concluded the first half with a procession of "Beauty through the Ages" or "Famous Lovers", and sometimes of such difficult subjects as "Famous Buildings". I clearly remember seeing a procession of "Famous Bridges" in a revue at the Chelsea Palace—and also a fine burlesque of such processions in one of the Farjeon revues. Up to 1939 the procession of rivers would have been as clearly understood as it was in 1779. But *One Night in Paris* and *Sous le Rideau* (*Under the Curtain*) were killed by the war, and when the Old Vic revived *The Critic* in 1945–6 the rivers and Britannia were unhappily, but perhaps reasonably, omitted. The procession remains a part of the burlesque tradition, but it will not come into its own again until the return of a more lavish age. Today, with many other theatrical traditions, the procession is lovingly preserved in the pantomime, where a finale without one would justly be considered an outrage.

Sheridan inherited a great part of the burlesque tradition; but what he inherited he perfected, and like all the great burlesque writers he added his own contributions to the tradition—processions and the patriotic joke in particular. The critics of his own time remarked on his ridicule of commencements, stage situations, and processions. Looking back at *The Critic* from a distance of nearly a century and three-quarters, it appears chiefly remarkable for its admirable restraint. Here is the perfection of mock-serious writing—the poker face and the unwinking eye.

JOHN HOOKHAM FRERE AND GEORGE CANNING

The Critic came appositely, like a summary, at the end of an era. The great poets might continue to write tragedies for reading at home, but in the theatre tragedy was dead. Its place was being taken by "drama", by plays of romance and sentiment —some made at home like *The Sicilian Romance*: or, *The Apparition of the Cliffs* (1794) adapted by Henry Siddons from Mrs. Radcliffe's novel; *The Smugglers* (1796) by Samuel Birch; *The Iron Chest* (1796) by George Colman the younger: others translated from the German of Schiller, Goethe, or Kotzebue: others partly derived from German sources, like M. G. Lewis's famous play, *The Castle Spectre* (1797). The sensational drama had arrived, and it was to hold the English stage from the end of the 18th to the beginning of the 20th century—first with its dungeons, spectres, lost heirs, and hidden wills; then, set to music, with its wicked squires, maidens and mortgages; and eventually, magnificently mounted, with its sealed orders, unscrupulous diplomats and gambling duchesses. Once again Vice and Virtue were opposed to each other—but in a fresh set of conventions. Plots became darkly entangled, theatrical effects brilliantly complicated, characters more than ever clear-cut, white and black. Sentimentality directed the actions of the just; implacable hatreds corroded the hearts of the proud.

O my gallant father! in what latitude of the ocean art thou now fondly dreaming of thy Stella, whom thou hast so oft indulg'd in all the sweet play of the heart? Could'st thou know thy honour was thy only wealth, rich in thyself, thou yet would'st weep for me—but no—around thy laurel'd couch I'd take my daily stand, teach thy full heart to cast its cares away, and smile content and happiness around thee.

It is the heroine of *The Smugglers* who is speaking, and she goes on like that throughout the whole play.

What, see a poor creature expiring for food, and not stretch forth a hand to save him! a seaman's daughter too, whose father at this moment may need the same at others hands—O no! I must indulge the sacred impulse.[1]

It is difficult to select from all this richness, sliding so easily from verse to prose, and back again to verse.

Unpitying censure marks the female's path with such insatiate eye, that half the benevolent purposes of the heart are frustrated thro' fear of forfeiting what the world calls character, and Pity's self is bound in Slander's chain.

The whole breed of sensational drama is coloured with this humourlessness. In *The Purse or the Benevolent Tar* (1794), by James C. Cross, it is without a shadow of a smile that the thief remarks: "The Baron's partiality must decrease, when he discovers the embezzlement." And *The Old Oak Chest* an anonymous play of 1816 contains lines which might have been a burlesque of themselves.

Adriana! is all safe?
My love, no; I hear a rustling in the bushes; concealment is again requisite.

Long before anyone thought of laughing at the English melodrama, the sensational and romantic drama of Germany attracted the wit of John Hookham Frere and George Canning in *The Anti-Jacobin*. Their famous outline of a drama, *The Rovers; or The Double Arrangement* (1798) was a composite burlesque of Goethe's *Stella* and Schiller's *The Robbers*, with glances at other plays by Kotzebue. The joke was partly directed against the badness of the English translations; but no merit in the originals could disguise the fact that the German plays did contain a high proportion of burlesqueable material.[2] Where heroes had once called to the clouds for vengeance and heroines

---

[1] That the poor creature is none other than the heroine's father, will not come as a surprise to connoisseurs of this style of writing.

[2] Another skit, *The Benevolent Cut-Throat*, "a play in seven acts, translated from the original of Klotzboggenhaggen", was printed in *The Meteors* (1799–1800).

THE AUTHOR

Richard Suett as Bayes

Engraving after a painting by John Graham

THE TWO MAN ARMY JOKE
From a woodcut in George Cruikshank's edition of 'Bombastes Furioso'

THE AUTHOR

Richard Suett as Bayes

Engraving after a painting by John Graham

THE GHOST

King Arthur and the Ghost of Gaffer Thumb

From a woodcut by George Cruikshank

MISS ROSE IN THE PART OF TOM THUMB
From a painting by John Berridge

MURDER AND SUICIDE

The last scene of *Tom Thumb* at the Scarborough Theatre

From a water-colour drawing by Thomas Rowlandson

THE PRISON SCENE

Design for the original frontispiece of *Chrononhotonthologos*
Attributed to Henri Gravelot

POMPOSITY

Charles Mathews as Sir Fretful Plagiary

From a water-colour drawing by Samuel de Wilde

THE THINKING ACTOR

Sir Ralph Richardson as Burleigh and Sir Laurence Olivier as Puff
in the Old Vic production of *The Critic*, 1945–6

TROUBLE WITH THE SCENERY

Sir Laurence Olivier as Puff at the rehearsal of *The Spanish Armada*

THE STAGE SAILOR
From a woodcut in 'George Cruikshank's Table Book'

THE TWO MAN ARMY JOKE
From a woodcut in George Cruikshank's edition of 'Bombastes Furioso'

ASPECTS OF THE MELODRAMA

Heroine, Countryman, and Village Squire

From a woodcut in 'George Cruikshank's Table Book'

BURLESQUE OF THE BALLET
From a water-colour drawing by Thomas Rowlandson

gone stark mad in white satin, the new drama propounded a spate of protestations, renunciations and reconciliations. Where problems had once been simple, the new drama propounded a confusion in married relationships unparalleled by any triangle play of the 20th century.

In Kotzebue's *Count Benyowsky* the governor's daughter proposes to escape with her father's prisoner, the married Benyowsky, upon the following exceptional understanding.

ATHANASIA: Pure and guiltless is my love for you—it is the affection
    of a sister towards a brother. No, I will not forsake you
    —I cannot forsake you. I will go with you into the wide
    world. I will witness the delight of your Emilia at your
    return. A beam of joy again warms my heart. I myself
    will conduct you to her arms. I will find my peace in
    yours—assist your wife in conducting your household—
    teach your babes to lisp your name. . . .

Persisting in this singular resolution, Athanasia accompanies Benyowsky to his ship. But the reproaches of her father, and the conflict between love and duty, are too much for her. She swoons; and Benyowsky rather ungallantly takes the opportunity to restore her to the Governor.

BENYOWSKY (*is extremely agitated, and lays* ATHANASIA, *still insensible,*
    in the arms of her father): Take her, old man.—(*Draws*
    out a picture of his wife.) Emilia! My wife!—To the vessel
    instantly! (*A confused noise takes place, and all hasten on*
    board.)
GOVERNOR (*pressing his daughter to his bosom with his left hand, while*
    he stretches forth the other towards the vessel): God bless
    thee, stranger. God bless thee!

All these German plays are concerned with some unreasonable relationship. In Kotzebue's famous play, *The Stranger*, the erring Mrs. Haller is happily restored to her husband after the exchange of a few high sentiments; and in *Lover's Vows*, Baron Wildenhain readily reunites himself to the mother of his natural son, though she is beneath him in station and he has not seen her for about twenty years. The furthest confine of improbability is reached in Goethe's *Stella* where a man who has deserted one wife for another is ecstatically claimed by both, and the curtain falls upon what appears to be a general consent for an establishment *à trois*.

CECILIA: Divide with me that heart, Stella, the whole of which
            belongs to you. You have saved my husband—saved
            him from himself, and you restore him to me again.
FERDINAND (*approaches* STELLA): My Stella!
STELLA: I comprehend it not.
CECILIA: You will know all—even now your heart explains it!
STELLA (*falling on* FERDINAND's *neck*): And may I trust that heart?
CECILIA: Do you thank me for arresting the fugitive?
STELLA (*taking* CECILIA *in her arms*): O Cecilia!
FERDINAND (*embracing both*): Mine! Mine!
STELLA (*taking hold of his hands and hanging upon him*): I am thine!
CECILIA: We are both thine!

In addition to the expected triangular problem, Schiller's
The Robbers is remarkable for an immensely involved plot with
a morbid parricide, a prisoner in a ruined tower, and scenes of
rapine and debauchery in town and forest. The scale of the
work is enormous, and indeed at its first publication it was
described by Schiller as a narrative work in which "advantage
has been taken of the *dramatic* method, without otherwise con-
forming to the stringent rules of theatrical composition, or
seeking the dubious advantage of stage adaptation".[1]

It was these two elements of the German play, the involved-
ness and the triangular relationships, that the authors of *The
Rovers* set out to enjoy.

It is remarkable that so sure a place in the history of burlesque should have been won by a work which appeared only
in a periodical, was not intended for performance,[2] and had
reference to works which, though frequently translated, were
for the most part still unperformed in the English theatre.[3]
The Rovers achieved its position because of its wit; because it
was acutely critical; and because it made new additions to the
burlesque tradition. It was the first burlesque in the romantic

---

[1] The 3rd Edition was the acting edition.

[2] In 1811 George Colman adapted *The Rovers* for the theatre as *The
Quadrupeds of Quedlinburgh*, to include a burlesque of *Pizarro* and of the
animals then crowding the stage at Covent Garden in *Timour the Tartar*.

[3] *The Rovers* was published in June 1798. *The Stranger* had been performed
at Drury Lane in March. Privately performed in 1798, *The Robbers* was not
acted publicly till 1799—and then in a heavily adapted version. *Lovers Vows*
was acted at Covent Garden in October 1798, five months after the appearance of *The Rovers*.

dramatic manner as opposed to the tragic, and it originated the literary joke of the portentous stage direction. The German plays were much burdened with directions, sometimes short but difficult of performance like "the colour rises to her cheeks"; sometimes plain but covering a prodigious field of action.

Grigori *attacks* Benyowsky *from behind. At the very moment appears* Kasarinoff *leading his two* Children. *He leaves them, fells* Tschulosnikoff *to the earth, and disarms him.* Benyowsky, *in the mean time, disarms* Grigori, *and holds him fast.* Tschulosnikoff *raves, shouts, and curses.* Theodora *appears on the balcony, mixes her shrieks with the various cries of the combatants, and runs back.*

Sometimes the direction suggests behaviour which seems too protracted to be of real value to the scene.

She sinks devoid of strength into a chair. Benyowsky *leans against the wall and hides his face. A long pause ensues. Athanasia's bosom heaves, and she appears to be contending with herself. At length she rises with a resolute air.*

In the minutely catalogued stage directions of *The Rovers* Frere and Canning contrived a double burlesque. It was a hit at stage directions in general; it was also the ideal way of burlesquing in a small space the elaborate plot and vast machinery of *The Robbers*.

Scene changes to the outside of the Abbey.—A Summer's Evening; Moonlight.
Companies of Austrian and Prussian Grenadiers march across the stage confusedly, as if returning from the Seven Years War.—Shouts and martial music.
The Abbey Gates are opened; the Monks are seen passing in procession, with the Prior at their head; the choir is heard chanting vespers; then a bell is heard, as if ringing for supper; soon after, a noise of singing and jollity. . . .

"As if returning from the Seven Years War". It is an admirable witticism and a new one. A hundred years later Max Beerbohm was to re-create it, and build upon it in the opulent stage-directions of *Savonarola*.

(Re-enter Guelfs and Ghibellines fighting. SAV. *and* LUC. *are arrested by Papal officers. Enter* MICHAEL ANGELO. ANDREA DEL SARTO *appears for a moment at the window.* PIPPA *passes. Brothers of the Misericordia go*

by, singing a Requiem for Francesca da Rimini. Enter BOCCACCIO, BEN-
VENUTO CELLINI, *and many others, making remarks highly characteristic
of themselves but scarcely audible through the terrific thunderstorm which
now bursts over Florence and is at its loudest and darkest crisis as the Curtain
falls.*)

Also in general burlesque of *The Robbers* is Rogero's soliloquy
in the dungeon. As a change from the operatic joke enjoyed by
Gay and Carey, Frere and Canning discovered a new target in
the dismal terrors of the Gothic drama. The scene is "*a subter-
ranean vault in the Abbey of Quedlinburgh, with coffins, 'scutcheons,
death's heads and crossbones—toads and other loathsome reptiles are
seen traversing the obscurer parts of the stage*". After "*a long silence,
during which the wind is heard to whistle through the caverns*", Rogero
advances and speaks.

ROGERO: Eleven years! it is now eleven years since I was first
immured in this living sepulchre—the cruelty of a Minister
—the perfidy of a Monk—Yes, Matilda! for thy sake—
alive amidst the dead—chained—coffined—confined—
cut off from the converse of my fellow-men. Soft!—what
have we here! (*Stumbles over a bundle of sticks.*) This cavern
is so dark that I can scarcely distinguish the objects under
my feet. Oh—the register of my captivity. Let me see;
how stands the account? (*Takes up the sticks, and turns them
over with a melancholy air; then stands silent for a few minutes,
as if absorbed in calculation.*)—Eleven years and fifteen days!
Hah! The twenty-eighth of August! How does the recollection of it vibrate on my heart!

It vibrates to the tune of a full long page of reminiscence, and
then, announcing that "despair sits brooding over the putrid
eggs of hope", concludes with a cue for song as blandly contrived as Mr. Lenville's in *Nicholas Nickleby*.[1]

Soft, what air was that? it seemed a sound of more than human
warblings. Again! (*listens attentively for some minutes.*) Only the wind;
it is well, however; it reminds me of that melancholy air, which has
so often solaced the hours of my captivity. Let me see whether the
damps of this dungeon have not yet injured my guitar. (*Takes his
guitar, tunes it, and begins the following air, with a full accompaniment
of violins from the orchestra.*)

[1] See p. 4.

And then follows the famous song by Canning, beginning

> Whene'er with haggard eyes I view
> This dungeon that I'm rotting in,
> I think of those companions true
> Who studied with me at the U-
>   -niversity of Gottingen—
>   -niversity of Gottingen.

The principal burlesque of *Stella* hits at the scene where Cecilia and Stella agree to eternal friendship within a few minutes of their first encounter. Frere's parallel scene between Matilda Pottingen and Cecilia Mückenfeld is excellent—but better still is a subtle joke about food which runs through the whole of the opening scene. In the first act of *Stella* the landlady is abnormally solicitous about serving dinner. In the first scene of *The Rovers* the subject of food pervades everything. It strays into the stage directions—(LANDLADY *enters, and places a leg of mutton on the table, with sour krout and prune sauce; then a small dish of black puddings.* CECILIA *and* MATILDA *appear to take no notice of her.*) It is also made the theme of Matilda's opening speech.

MATILDA: Is it possible for me to have dinner sooner?
LANDLADY: Madam, the Brunswick post-waggon is not yet come in, and the ordinary is never before two o'clock.
MATILDA: (*with a look expressive of disappointment, but immediately recomposing herself.*) Well, then, I must have patience. (*Exit* LANDLADY.) O Casimere!—How often have the thoughts of thee served to amuse these moments of expectation!—What a difference, alas!—Dinner—it is taken away as soon as over, and we regret it not!—It returns again with the return of appetite.—The beef of tomorrow will succeed to the mutton of today, as the mutton of today succeeded to the veal of yesterday. But when once the heart has been occupied by a beloved object, in vain would we attempt to supply the chasm by another. How easily are our desires transferred from dish to dish!—Love only, dear, delusive, delightful love, restrains our wandering appetites, and confines them to a particular gratification!
                [*Post-horn blows; re-enter* LANDLADY.
LANDLADY: Madam, the post-waggon is just come in with only a single gentlewoman.

MATILDA: Then show her up—and let us have dinner instantly;
(LANDLADY *going*)—and remember—(*after a moment's
recollection, and with great earnestness*)—remember the
toasted cheese.   [*Exit* LANDLADY.

Finally it becomes the subject of a magnificent piece of nonsense, which is one of the best things in the whole burlesque.
The shuttlecock of platitude at the end of this passage, is in
criticism of similar blunt exchanges in the plays of Kotzebue.

LANDLADY: Have you carried the dinner to the prisoner in the vaults
of the abbey?
WAITER: Yes—Pease soup as usual—with the scrag end of a neck
of mutton. The emissary of the Count was here again
this morning, and offered me a large sum of money if
I would consent to poison him.
LANDLADY: Which you refused? (*with hesitation and anxiety*).
WAITER: Can you doubt it? (*with indignation*).
LANDLADY (*recovering herself, and drawing up with an expression of
dignity*): The conscience of a poor man is as valuable
to him as that of a prince . . .
WAITER: It ought to be still more so, in proportion as it is gener-
ally more pure.
LANDLADY: Thou say'st truly Job.
WAITER (*with enthusiasm*): He who can spurn at wealth when offered
as the price of crime, is greater than a prince.

At the end of the scene, when Casimere has arrived and
discovered that Matilda is in the house, he bids the landlady
call her "Instantly—instantly—tell her her loved, her long-lost
—tell her——" "Shall I tell her dinner is ready?" says the
landlady, faithful to her office to the last line of her part.
Food was a traditional joke of the English pantomime. It had
been talked about and served in many earlier burlesques. But
it had not before this been made the subject of a first-rate
critical joke. Henceforward food on the stage becomes a part
of the burlesque inheritance. Thomas Dibdin has a variant of
the joke in *Bonifacio and Bridgetina* (1808) in the hermit who
is not "anxious for paltry food", but who, none the less, takes
eager notice of the basket brought daily from the village. Gilbert reconstructs it again in *Ruddigore* (1887) where Rose
Maybud discovers a charitable purpose in an apple.

A maiden, and in tears? Can I do aught to soften thy sorrow?
This apple—

And if Stephen Leacock did not intentionally build on Frere's
joke, he was certainly making an exactly similar point in his
burlesque Society drama *Behind the Beyond* (1913).

Sir John says to Lady Cecily—
"Shall I ring for tea?"
And Lady Cecily says—
"Thanks no," in a weary tone.

This shows that they are the kind of people who can have tea
at any time. All through a problem play it is understood that any
of the characters may ring for tea and get it. Tea in a problem play
is the same as whiskey in a melodrama.

In the second act of *Behind the Beyond* supper is served
("langouste aux champignons") and the tea, twice rejected in
the first act, is at last brought in to relieve the melancholy of
Act 3.

There was one joke in *The Rovers* which was both up-
to-date and traditional. The terrors of the Gothic drama provided a welcome excuse for reviving the Ghost. At the end of
the Prologue "*The Ghost of* PROLOGUE'S GRANDMOTHER *by the
Father's side, appears to soft music, in a white tiffany riding-hood.*
PROLOGUE *kneels to receive her blessing, which she gives in a solemn
and affecting manner, the audience clapping and crying all the while.—
Flash of lightning.*—PROLOGUE *and his* GRANDMOTHER *sink through
the trap-doors.*

THOMAS DIBDIN, CHARLES DICKENS, AND THE ENGLISH MELODRAMA

Ay, gnash your teeth as fiercely as you please—scatter fire and
destruction from your eyes—the fury of a woman piques my fancy
—it makes you more beautiful, more tempting.—Come, this
resistance will garnish my triumph, and your struggles give zest to
my embraces.—Come, come to my chamber—I burn with desire.
—Come this instant.

The sentiment will be familiar to every connoisseur of English
villainy—but this particular specimen of it comes from *The*

Robbers by Schiller. It is a proof of the hybrid descent of melodrama.

Melodrama (which is drama underlined and emotionalized by the addition of music) was imported from France in 1802, in *A Tale of Mystery* by Thomas Holcroft, founded upon Pixeré-court's *Coelina*. But *A Tale of Mystery* was performed in a theatre already deeply involved in sensationalism. The English melodrama derives partly from the French *mélodrame*; but it descends equally from the tremendous dumb-show dramas of the Royal Circus, from the German translations, and from the English "Tale of Terror", as purveyed by Mrs. Radcliffe, Monk Lewis, and a coven of imitators. Indeed it also derives from 18th century blank verse tragedy.

Thomas Dibdin in his *Reminiscences* (1827) gives an extraordinary account of the conversion of *Douglas* into a melodrama in 1819.

Mrs. Egerton performed Young Norval in 'Douglas'; which tragedy, without omitting a single line of the author, made a very splendid melodrame, with the additions of Lord Randolph's magnificent banquet, a martial Scotch dance, and a glee, formed from Home's words—

Free is his heart who for his country fights &c., &c.

exquisitely set . . . and delightfully sung, together with an expensive processional representation of the landing of the Danes: besides all this, as a Surrey Theatre gallery audience always expects some *ultra* incident, I had a representative of Lady Randolph in the person of a very clever boy, by whose good acting and fearless agility, the northern dame, at the conclusion of the tragedy, was seen to throw herself from a distant precipice into a boiling ocean, in a style which literally brought down thunders of applause.

Thomas Dibdin was an important figure in the history of melodrama, both as theatre manager and as author. He presented melodramas. He wrote them. And he burlesqued them. His *Bonifacio and Bridgetina; or The Knight of the Hermitage, or the Windmill Turrett; or the Spectre of the North-East Gallery*, produced at Covent Garden in 1808, was one of the earliest melodrama burlesques.

The prelude to *Bonifacio and Bridgetina* is set in the corridor behind the boxes just before the beginning of the play, and presents a neat catalogue of the ingredients which Dibdin considered proper to melodrama.

AUTHOR: Are you fond of hermits?

MEDLEY: Very.

AUTHOR: I have a charming one, and introduce a dance in his solitary cell.

MEDLEY: That's surprising—but why?

AUTHOR: Why? Why because there *must* be a dance that's all.[1]

MEDLEY: A good reason—Have you any robbers?

AUTHOR: More than *forty*—and as sentimental a set of scoundrels as you'd wish to give your purse to.[2]

MEDLEY: The captain a hero in disguise?

AUTHOR: Yes, and in addition, combats, elopements, escapes, gigantic apparitions, and dear little children.

MEDLEY: Then what else *can* be wanting?

AUTHOR: Nothing but a conflagration in the last scene; the combustibles for which are in preparation at this very moment.

MEDLEY: Such things should finish with a conflagration; but how d'ye put it out?

AUTHOR: Can't you guess?

MEDLEY: No.

AUTHOR: No! then you shall own this to be the most surprising thing of all, and only reserved for this age to accomplish. We absolutely mean to extinguish it with *real water*.

MEDLEY: Extinguish fire with real water! My dear boy, let me embrace you.

This is entirely in the best tradition of irony—the manner derived from Bayes, and the matter from the contemporary theatre. The play is not as good as the prelude, but it does not belie the author's generous promises, and in one or two places there is dialogue of an excellent burlesque flavour. For instance, the villainous Sacripando's address to the heroine:

I'll shut thee in the haunted windmill tower, feed thee on bread and water, and thy son shall instant perish—if all this

---

[1] Compare the views of Bayes in *The Rehearsal* and of Mr. Folair and Mr. Lenville in *Nicholas Nickleby*. The oddest example of a dance dragged in must be that at the end of *The Beaux' Stratagem*, which takes place in the middle of the night after the house has been raised by burglars.

[2] *The Forty Thieves* had been produced at Drury Lane in 1806.

does not convince thee how I love thee, thou hast a heart of adamant.

And the heroine's reflection after being confined in the windmill:

I declare upon my honour, if the balcony was a little lower, I'd throw myself down, and be dashed to pieces, before I'd put up with this usage.

Both these remarks foreshadow the straight-faced nonsense which Stephen Leacock was to employ so successfully a century later.

Six years earlier Dibdin had written *Harlequin Habeas, or The Hall of Spectres* for the Covent Garden pantomime of Christmas 1802. In this "the ghosts in 'Hamlet', 'Don Juan', 'Blue Beard', the 'Castle Spectre', and other popularly terrific dramas were successfully introduced". The comic ghost (Fielding's favourite joke and a permanent character in *Punch and Judy*) is still seen from time to time in modern pantomimes. The gag usually consists in leaving the dame, or an ugly sister, sitting beside the ghost, whom she supposes, for a few delightful moments, to be somebody else. It is reasonable to conjecture that this familiar jest has a long pedigree.

Certain aspects of the melodrama were evidently burlesqued at a very early date, and the ghost, honoured veteran of the tradition, was an obvious choice. But perhaps the melodrama was too popular, at that time, to be held up to full-length ridicule. *Bonifacio and Bridgetina* was a failure. Dibdin had founded it on a French burlesque—"a very sensible and whimsical satire on the great rage (then at its height) for melodramas ... But the joke was not taken ... and, after a few nights my bombastic hero died a natural death; I got nothing from the theatre for his short life, and lost money by printing the piece".

Dibdin's other burlesques are disappointing. *Melodrama Mad* (1819) is a mysterious piece with no apparent bearing on the subject of melodrama. *The Seven Champions of Christendom* (1821); *Leonora; or The Apparition on the White Horse; or Love in all its Horrors* (1821) and *Peggy Larkins* (1826) are not in the British Museum or the Larpent collection, either in print or manuscript. *Don Giovanni*, the hit of the season at the Surrey in 1817, was not a true burlesque.[1] Described as a "Comic, Heroic, Operatic, Tragic, Pantomimic, Burletta—Spectacular Extravaganza", it is an early example of the facetious rhymed couplet travesty, which was to usurp the throne of burlesque, and to borrow its name for a great part of the 19th century. It is chiefly interesting as a reminder that the extravaganza did not originate with Planché. Twenty years later, Dibdin's last work, *Alexander the Great! in Little* (1837) was equally in the extravaganza style.

An examination of the descent and growth of the English melodrama would require a separate volume.[2] For the purpose of this work it is only necessary to notice the astonishing vigour of the thing. Whether in mouldering castle with midnight spectre and sliding panel, or in cottage home with the snow falling on the mortgaged roof, there is never the least abatement of spirit, language or action.

As an example of domestic melodrama, with humble virtue too plainly destined for severe trials, take this opening dialogue from *Holly Bush Hall* by W. E. Suter (1860). Dame Acton and May are discussing the inclemency of the weather.

DAME ACTON: How the wind howls and moans about our poor old homestead—and how heavily the snow is falling! most appalling are the wild terrors of the night! Five miles from the sea though we are, I can hear the wild foam dashing on the rocks. Oh, what a night is this for the homeless and the friendless.

MAY: It is indeed, Mother; Heaven help them all! The hollows on these downs are terrible dangers to all wayfarers on such a night as this.

—So terrible, indeed, that May can only trust herself to describe them in song.

> 'Midst the wild falling snow,
> Those wretches now shrinking,
> With shrieks and with cries so forlorn—

---

[1] "I saw Mozart's opera on a Tuesday", he wrote in his *Reminiscences*; ". . . I had finished the first act late on the Saturday night". Less than a fortnight after he had seen the opera, the piece was produced at the Surrey, where it ran for a hundred nights.

[2] Maurice Willson Disher's *Blood and Thunder* (1949), published after this section had been written, is the latest and best study of melodrama.

Oh may Heaven protect them, or they perish
In their cold bed slow sinking!
This terrible storm!

After which a knocking at the door announces the return of
the prodigal son, hotly pursued by the Sussex police.

The weather was always important in melodrama. Apart
from its value to the plot, it served as a background and a contrast to the gentleness and goodness of the girls. In *The Pilot* by
Edward Fitzball (1825) Kate and Caecilia stand by the window
watching the ship in the storm. "There she moves once more,"
says Kate. "I dare not trust myself to gaze further lest the faint
ray of hope which that one glimpse instilled into my bosom be
for ever changed to despair. O man! man! when sorrow and
calamity surround thee, woman's last, best effort to assist thy
drooping fortune still remains forcibly in her heart, and still
reaches thee in her prayers". Thunder and lightning are succeeded by "Storm Music" and off go Kate and Caecilia in a
duet called "Heaven shield the mariner in his path of storms".

It was in *The Pilot* that T. P. Cooke made such a hit as Long
Tom Coffin. At the end of the play Long Tom throws himself
at the American captain's feet and intercedes for the Englishman, Barnstaple. But Barnstaple rejects this behaviour. "Tom
Coffin," he cries, "up, up; is this a position for a British
seaman?"

Acting which got away with that kind of stuff must have been
tremendously convincing. No-one today could hold an audience
silent during such a scene as this, for instance, from Buckstone's
Luke the Labourer (1826).

SQUIRE: Well Clara, and how is your father?
CLARA: He's very—that is, but poorly, sir.
SQUIRE: Come hither, Clara; let me speak to you alone. (*The rest
retire.*) Your father is in difficulties, I understand.
CLARA. He is indeed, sir.
SQUIRE: I'm very sorry: but if you will come to the Manor House,
this evening, I shall be at leisure, and will give you my
assistance and advice.

As an example of the garrulous monologue with action, this
portion of a speech from *Alice Gray* (1839) by John T. Haines,
is particularly impressive.

... Yes, yes, I was wicked to wish to die while he is in prison, with no-one to take him a morsel of food—time will prove my innocence. I will hope—I will hope yet! I will take him his dinner to the gaol, he said he was hungry, and (*starts, on seeing the table*) Gone—gone! the only food we had! Oh, this is cruel! but what, what *can* I do? He will starve before my eyes, and I *can* save him! Yes, I will not think—but Heaven will forgive me for praying for death, before I leave the church. Harry, should you ever come back, then you—ha! (*stands for a moment transfixed as . . . she raises her eyes to the portrait, and sees the locket.*) The locket! my mother's locket! (*darts to it and clutches it.*) It is! What thought flashes like a lightning stroke across my brain? (*speaks rapidly*) This was locked up with my uncle's money, and was stolen with it! it may point the thief, it may. (*pauses to think*) I'll fly to a magistrate—yes, it will clear my name! Blessed proof, it will secure the miscreant. Heaven aid me—my strength falters—heart bear up till all is over—burst—burst then —burst then—I shall be happy. (*rushes frantically out.*)

It bears no resemblance to human behaviour—but the roars of applause that such an exit undoubtedly commanded, were well earned. That was the stuff and those were the days.

To the 20th century every aspect of the melodrama appears funny. Who could refrain from burlesquing it? The answer is that the early Victorian dramatists could. In its heyday the melodrama was a splendid entertainment; people enjoyed it as it was. Besides, the humorists were otherwise engaged, rocking with laughter at each other's puns, and writing facetious travesties of the world's noblest tragedies. It was not the dramatists, but the novelists, who disclosed the hidden humours of the melodrama. The whole of the Crummles episodes in *Nicholas Nickleby* are a burlesque of the melodramatic theatre, from Mr. Lenville's brief proposals for the introduction of a dance for the Phenomenon and Mr. Folair, to the complete description of that romantic drama which Nicholas saw on the night after he joined the Crummles company, and in which Smike made his first appearance on the stage "with another gentleman as a general rebellion". Nor did the ebullient humour of Charles Dickens lead him into half as much exaggeration as the 20th century ignorantly supposes. Anyone acquainted with early 19th century drama will recognize Mr. Crummles's play as a fair specimen of the period, twisted askew just sufficiently for the creation of a great burlesque joke.

The Mortal Struggle (for such the play must have been) [1] was a melodrama in the early tradition of the "Tale of Terror". At Miss Snevellicci's great bespeak, not long afterwards, it was the more up-to-date domestic melodrama which the Crummles Company performed in the translation from the French by Nicholas Nickleby. The plot is not as fully described as that of *The Mortal Struggle*, but it will be recognized immediately for what it is.

But when Nicholas came on for his crack scene with Mrs. Crummles, what a clapping of hands there was! When Mrs. Crummles (who was his unworthy mother) sneered, and called him "presumptuous boy", and he defied her, what a tumult of applause came on! When he quarrelled with the other gentleman about the young lady, and producing a case of pistols, said, that if he *was* a gentleman he would fight him in that drawing-room, until the furniture was sprinkled with the blood of one, if not two—how boxes, pit and gallery, joined in one most vigorous cheer! When he called his mother names, because she wouldn't give up the young lady's property, and she relenting, caused him to relent likewise, and fall down on one knee and ask her blessing, how the ladies in the audience sobbed! When he was hid behind the curtain in the dark, and the wicked relation poked a sharp sword in every direction save where his legs were plainly visible, what a thrill of anxious fear ran through the house! . . . And when, at last, in the pump-and-tub scene, Mrs. Grudden lighted the blue fire, and all the unemployed members of the company came in, and tumbled down in various directions—not because that had anything to do with the plot, but in order to finish off with a tableau—the audience (who had by this time increased considerably) gave vent to such a shout of enthusiasm, as had not been heard in those walls for many and many a day.

Dickens described the plot, Thackeray described the manner of melodrama. *The Rose and The Ring* (1854) was called 'a fireside pantomime' by its author. More exactly, it was a burlesque of a melodrama tricked out as a fairy story. Here is the little child cast out in the snow; the heir deprived, the usurping uncle, the recognition scene, and virtue triumphant: and, although the royal habit of speaking in concealed blank verse,

---

[1] The other two plays called for rehearsal by Mr. Crummles at 10 o'clock, *Ways and Means* and *Intrigue*, are by George Colman and John Poole, and do not fit the description.

is, in one sense, a continuation of an older tradition, yet—
allowing a wicked monarch in place of the regulation squire—
the language of King Valoroso is the language of melodrama.
"Why did I steal my nephew's, my young Giglio's—? Steal!
said I? no, no, no, not steal, not steal. Let me withdraw that
odious expression. I took, and on my manly head I set, the
royal crown of Paflagonia . . ."

Here too is an early example of the famous joke of melodramatic enunciation. "R-r-r-r-Rejected! Fiends and perdition! The bold Hogginarmo rejected! All the world shall hear
of my rage; and you, madam, you above all shall rue it." That
empty threat upon the exit line is another melodramatic tradition, still maintained in the prologue of any pantomime worthy
of its ancestors.

Finally, the language of King Padella (who also speaks in
royal verse under the pressure of intense emotion), displays
the demoniac rage and the traditional laugh of abandoned
villainy.

Whip, whack, flog, starve, rack, punish, torture Bulbo—break all
his bones—roast him or flay him alive—pull all his pretty teeth
out one by one! but justly dear as Bulbo is to me,—Joy of my
eyes, fond treasure of my soul—Ha, ha, ha, ha! revenge is dearer
still. Ho! torturers, rack-men, executioners, light up the fires,
and make the pincers hot! Get lots of boiling lead! Bring out
ROSALBA!

It was not in the nature of extravaganza to create anything
so good as this. Not even the famous old thriller, *The Miller and
his Men*, could inspire Francis Talfourd and Henry J. Byron to
write anything better than the usual facetiousness in their new
"mealy-drama" produced in 1860.

> Confusion!
> > Ditto!
> > > Foiled!
> > > > Destruction!
> > > > > True!
> Cuss everything!
> > > I quite agree with you!

Apart from a few such hits at melodramatic anger, the play just twaddles on with lines like—

> The man I *loathe there!*
>> Ha! Hall*o* there!
>>> *Lo, there!*
> I see *Lothair!*
>> Then we had best not go there.

There are plenty of stage directions for "melodrama music", and, no doubt, there was much burlesque in the acting of the piece: but the writing is pure travesty. It is not melodrama criticized, but merely the plot of melodrama retold and mis-used. The extravaganza writers were enslaved by the rhymed couplet and the diligent pursuit of an ancient joke prevented their enjoyment of a contemporary one.

For several years, however, a re-action against this false conception of burlesque had been gathering strength,[1] and, not long after *The Miller and his Men*, Lacy began to publish little burlesques in what was called a "Sensation Series". They are not very good, but they come as a breath of fresh air after the long tyranny of the extravaganzas.

Here is Burnand in *The Siege of Seringapatam* (1863) with the pleasant stage direction, "Exeunt the entire British Army". Here is *The Tyrant! The Slave!! The Victim!!! and the Tar!!!!* (1864, by Burnand?) with some fine seafaring language for Jack Shivertimbers. "Sluice my topgallant boom!" and "Splice my quarterdeck!" are better than a page full of puns; and "the lubber who wouldn't assist a lovely woman in distress is un-worthy of the name of a British tar", is an early expression of a sentiment justly famous in the burlesque tradition. Eighteen years later it was to turn up in *Iolanthe*. "Well, ma'am," says Private Willis to the Fairy Queen, "I don't think much of the British soldier who wouldn't ill-convenience himself to save a female in distress."

The serious origin of this joke is contained in three lines of *The Honey Moon*, a play by John Tobin, produced in 1805.

---

[1] See pp. 111 and 115.

The man that lays his hand upon a woman,
Save in the way of kindness, is a wretch,
Whom't were gross flattery to name a coward—

a precept highly agreeable to the age of melodrama, and one which sagacious dramatists had echoed again and again. As a young man, Edward Fitzball was engaged to enliven the English text of *The Somnambulist*, and he remarks in his autobiography (1859) with the air of a man who had, once upon a time, engaged in a very old trick: "At length, at the scene where the Count goes out at the window, and where I had contrived to pop into his mouth a clap-trap, respecting what the man deserves who would be coward enough to take advantage of unprotected female innocence, Elliston smiled one of his George-the-Fourth smiles, and exclaimed, rubbing his hands, exultingly,—'That will do, sir, that will do; now we *shall* bring them down!'"

Sentiments which had once provoked Sheridan's satire, had become clap-trap to the young Edward Fitzball. And clap-trap is never long in exciting its deserved reply.

It was, perhaps, Thackeray who first deflated Tobin's golden precept, by quoting it solemnly in *The Rose and The Ring*. "As England's poesy has well remarked," observes Prince Giglio, " 'The man that lays his hand upon a woman, save in the way of kindness, is a villain'." Certainly, from that time onwards, the phrase, with many variants, has been a favoured ornament of English burlesque.

The Rosebud of Stingingnettle Farm (1862) by Henry J. Byron is not very funny, but it is interesting to find an arch-extravaganza writer altering his style and producing new examples of the joke of enunciation. The wicked squire says "*Te*remble!" In *Bonifacio and Bridgetina* Thomas Dibdin included "dear little children" in his list of good things. In *Alice, the Mystery or the Parentless Maiden of the Cottage on the Cliff* (1865), by John Smith, we have the "che-i-ld", and spelt so too.

From the 1860's onwards the melodrama is anybody's game, but no-one produced anything critical enough or witty enough to stand beside the great works of the burlesque tradition. The bigness of the melodrama seemed to defy the burlesquer. Anyone could make a skit on the wicked baronet, and the mother and child cast out in the snow; [1] but a thing which all did fairly well, nobody did superlatively well. Not even Gilbert, in spite of *H.M.S. Pinafore* and *Ruddigore*. Not even Shaw: *Poison, Passion and Petrification* (1905) is merely high jinks, and scores no critical point at all. It was to be left to Stephen Leacock to make the best critical comment on melodrama since Dickens.

THE JOLLY JACK TAR JOKE

THAT noblest creature of the English melodrama, the jolly jack tar, demands a section, or, as he would certainly have said, a log-book, to himself. He was not a character of the Elizabethan or Jacobean theatres. *The Fair Maid of the West* by Thomas Heywood (1630) is full of sailors, but

> Aboard, aboard! the wind stands fair for England;
> The ships have all weighed anchor—

is the saltest part of their conversation, and not one of them has a better name than "1st Captain" or "2nd Sailor". Ben, in Congreve's *Love for Love* (1695), was the original sailor with a gay heart and a strange vocabulary. But Ben was not good, and his metaphor was not in the least romantic. "You're a tight vessel, and well rigged, an you were but as well manned," he says to Mrs. Frail within two minutes of meeting her. And he quarrels with Miss Prue and gets called a stinking tar-barrel. Ben was a live person not a type, a good sort not a hero.

Nor was there anything romantic about the sailors in *The Fair Quaker of Deal or The Humours of the Navy* by Charles Shadwell, produced at Drury Lane in February 1709/10, a rough comedy with the better characters bearing names like Worthy and Pleasant. Flip, the drunken commodore, has a little sea talk, but only a little, not more than phrases like "Talking to you is like Rowing against Wind and Tide, and therefore e'en Steer your Compass your own way". The rest of the talk is only language normal to any Restoration intrigue: the characters

---

[1] Mrs. Opie, in her novel *Father and Daughter*, created the first mother and child in the snow in 1801. They reached the English theatre in Moncrieff's version of this story at the Coburg theatre in 1820. See M. Willson Disher, *op. cit.*, pp. 84–5.

may be men of the sea, but the play is a comedy on shore, and is only interesting to this enquiry for the fact that one man bears a nautical name. The officer described as "a finical Sea-Fop, a mighty reformer of the Navy" is called Mizen—an early fore-father of all those nautical men with nautical names who were to throng the stage a century later.[1]

That name 'Mizen' is a slight glance toward the future—but the true sentimental, pure-minded, gallant, jolly jack tar, the famous theatrical type of the late 18th and early 19th centuries, was not to be found anywhere as early as 1710. He had some-thing of Congreve's Ben in his veins: he was in part derived from the simple hero of popular songs and ballads;[2] but his principal line of descent arose much later in the century—in the sailor characters in the novels of Tobias Smollett.

Smollett had served in the navy and his sea sketches in *Roderick Random* (1748) were drawn with the pen of authority. Others before him had introduced a smack of marine idiom: it was Smollett who made the first lively exposition of that salt sea lingo, which was soon to become a peculiarity of the English theatre. Lieut. Tom Bowling's conversation is couched in deep sea phrases; and an un-named sailor in the *Thunder* reports of a dying comrade, "It seems my poor mess-mate must part his cable for want of a little assistance. His fore-top-sail is loose already". And, later, "I hailed him several times, but he was too far on his way, and the enemy had got possession of his close quarters".

Three years later, in *Peregrine Pickle* (1751) the idiom of Hawser Trunnion and Jack Hatchway has become much more elaborate. There is considerable wit but little simplicity in

---

[1] Flip and Tom Cagg belong to the nomenclature of drink. Cagge is an early form of keg. When *The Fair Quaker* was revived in 1773, steps were taken to remedy a topical defect by adding the names of Binnacle and Hatchway to the persons of the drama.

[2] Not only rough songs; polished ones too, such as John Gay's "Sweet William's Farewell"

> All in the *Downs* the fleet was moor'd,
> The streamers waving in the wind,
> When black-ey'd *Susan* came aboard:—
> "Oh! where shall I my true love find!
> Tell me, ye jovial sailors! tell me true,
> If my sweet *William* sails among the crew."

Hatchway's letter reporting on the last illness of Peregrine's aunt.

Cousin Pickle,—and I hope you are in a better trim than your aunt, who hath been fast moored to her bed these seven weeks by several feet of under-water lodging in her hold and hollop, whereby I doubt her planks are rotted, so as she cannot choose but fall to pieces in a short time. I have done all in my power to keep her tight and easy and free from sudden squalls that might overstrain her; and here have been doctors, who have skuttled her lower deck, and let out six gallons of water. . . . [1]

These sea portraits of Smollett were something new and they possessed the minds of a people who were rapidly becoming sea-conscious and sailor-proud. One of those undoubtedly influenced by Smollett was Charles Dibdin, who paid him the compliment of borrowing the names of his characters. It was no plagiarism. It was the right thing to do. Jack Rattlin and Tom Bowling were just as well known as Jack Tar.

The great success which attended Dibdin's entertainments, and especially his sea songs, has rather left the impression that the theatre owes the jolly jack tar of the stage to him. To some extent it does: but Smollett was before him even on the stage, with *The Reprisal* or *The Tars of Old England*, produced at Drury Lane in 1757. It is a singularly silly play, but the plot was an early step in a famous direction, concerned as it is with the rescue of three English from a French ship through the intrepid conduct of Lieut. Lyon, Midshipman Haulyard, and Block, a seaman.

Garrick had taken the tip from Smollett a year and a half earlier still, when he spoke the prologue to Mallet's masque *Britannia* (May 1755) in the character of a drunken sailor. "It was delivered with the greatest humour," wrote Arthur Murphy, "and from the nature of the subject was so popular, that it was called for many nights after the *Masque* itself was

---

[1] Compare in *The Pickwick Papers*: "your farther had hopes as she vould have vorked round as usual but just as she was a turnen the corner my boy she took the wrong road and vent down hill vith a velocity you never see . . ." After nearly a hundred years of stage sailors, Tony Weller's letter on the death of his wife was a brilliant and welcome development in the whimsicalities of metaphor. But the connection between the two letters is obvious. Smollett was the strongest of Charles Dickens' literary godfathers.

laid aside, and Garrick was obliged, though he did not act in the play, to be in readiness to answer the public demand." [1]

Five years later, in 1760, Isaac Bickerstaffe's famous 'entertainment', *Thomas and Sally*, presented the familiar triangle of village maiden, importunate squire, and noble sailor.[2] And this too was before Dibdin's earliest work in the theatre.

The sea talk of Ben in *Love for Love* had been a fair reflection of his character. He spoke his mind and there was not the least difficulty in understanding his meaning. "A man that is married," he says, "is no more like another man than a gally-slave is like one of us free sailors: he is chained to an oar all his life; and, mayhap, forced to tug a leaky vessel into the bargain." In *Thomas and Sally* the sea-talk has become more formal, but it is modestly confined to remarks like "Avast!" and "Messmates, what cheer?", the most extravagant of Tom's observations being no worse than "weigh anchor, tack about and let's bear down". Nine years later, the conversation of Captain Ironsides in *The Brothers*—though perfectly intelligible—has become considerably more idiomatic, and, as though conscious of a possible danger, Cumberland makes Sir Richard Dove say, "A truce to your sea-phrases, for I don't understand them". And, indeed, it was not to be long before the sailor hero was stuck

---

[1] The prologue is printed in Murphy's biography of Garrick (1801), Vol. I, p. 270.

[2] The deathless phrase "A wife in every port" comes from *Thomas and Sally*. Thomas sings,

> How happy is the sailor's life,
> From coast to coast to roam;
> In every port he finds a wife,
> In every land a home.

And earlier in the piece Dorcas has referred to "one that gets a wife at ev'ry port". *The Oxford Dictionary of Quotations* (up to 1951) has allowed the phrase to Charles Dibdin, who borrowed it in 1790 for "Jack in his Element", a song in *The Wags*.

The sailor's reputation for unfaithfulness was doubtless an ancient joke. In *Dido and Aeneas* (1688–90) Nahum Tate had written :

> Come away, fellow Saylors your Anchors be weighing,
> Time and Tide will admit no delaying.
> Take a Bouze short leave of your Nymphs on the Shore,
> And Silence their Morning
> With Vows of returning,
> But never intending to Visit them more.

fast in the sands of metaphor. The victories of Hawke and
Rodney and Howe and Nelson created a demand for the sailor.
The public wanted him. The theatre managers needed him.
He was praised, he was flattered; he was spoilt. The carefree
rogue drawn by Congreve, the tough, honest fellow drawn by
Smollett, the engaging creature imagined by Garrick, Isaac
Bickerstaffe and Charles Dibdin—all disappear. In their place
arises a custodian of the nation's virtue, a tar without reproach,
and a jolly one into the bargain. A character has been con-
verted into a type. A man has been exchanged for a prig.

"If my little Sal, my pretty pinnace, sail but in smooth water,
my hearts timbers are as sound as ever; but if grief have shat-
tered her hulk, or she be foundered in a hard squall of adver-
sity, farewell to comfort." Will Steady in *The Purse; or The
Benevolent Tar* by J. C. Cross (1794) conducts his entire conversation in this bogus marine jargon, sometimes as soggy as this
complicated simile, and sometimes untranslatable bluster, like
"Damme! I'll snap your grappling irons short as a biscuit and
unship every headrail from larboard to starboard." [1]

The rot spread rapidly; in M. G. Lewis's *One O'clock or The
Knight and the Wood Demon* (1811) Rolf says to the terrified
Leolyn, "What, betray you? Boy, you are helpless and in dis-
tress! *She* is a woman, and *I* was for twelve years a Sailor!"

The jolly jack tar had become so firmly fixed in the English
theatre that, even when his sentiments had become as fatuous
as this, it was still a long time before anyone felt strong enough
to expose him. At last, in 1826, Frederic Reynolds, in his autobiography, objected violently to the modern "trap-clapping
sailors"—"impostors in a blue jacket, and trowsers, who vocifer-
ate a certain number of slang nautical phrases, who with their
elbows bang their tobacco boxes, put quids in their mouths,
pull up their trowsers, and boasting of 'Britannia's wooden
walls' and 'Albion's matchless glory' swagger up to the lamps

---

[1] See S. Birch's two plays *The Adopted Child* (1795) and *The Smugglers*
(1796) for similar dialogue. Lieut. Tom Bowling's ". . . if you come athwart
me, 'ware your gingerbread work, I'll be foul of your quarter, damn me
. . ." had been nearly as extravagant, but Bowling's lingo flows from a live
character; Will Steady has no character except that which the actor can
lend him. Fortunately for the author Steady was played by John Bannister,
famous in sailor parts. He also played Trim in *The Smugglers*, Harry Hawser,
Chearly, and many other salt-named characters.

exclaiming, 'There's a *sailor* for you' though every rational Englishman, ashamed of this libel on his countrymen, involuntarily retorts 'There's a *brute* for you' ".

Frederic Reynolds could say what he liked: the managers, and the public, knew better. 1825 had been the year of Edward Fitzball's phenomenally successful drama, *The Pilot*, with T. P. Cooke as Long Tom Coffin. In the year of Reynolds's autobiography Cooke was playing the sailor, Philip, in Buckstone's *Luke the Labourer*; and he was to go on playing magnificent sailors for the rest of his stage life—William in *Black Eyed Susan* by Douglas Jerrold in 1829; Harry Halliyard (the Pride of Battersea Hard) in *My Poll and My Partner Joe* by J. T. Haines in 1835; Mat Merriton in *The Ocean of Life* or *Every Inch a Sailor* by the same author in 1836. The character of the sailor hero was immutable. Only the name changed, from some salt sea virtue in one play to a fragment of nautical tackle in another. Mat Mainmast in 1803,[1] or Mat Spritsail in 1843,[2] it was all the same to the author, and all the same to the public. *William and Adelaide* (1830), "being exceedingly national and nautical", wrote Edward Fitzball, was "received with universal and marked applause, and ran the whole season". The public wanted plays about splendid sailors, and so long as they did so, no one was likely to dissect their extravagances. Not even in 1840 when J. P. Hart, in *Jane; the Licensed Victualler's Daughter*, converted his man from sail to steam. "Get in your coals," says Jemmy Filer, "oil your engine—heat your boiler, and when the steam is up, the parson shall throw us into gear, and away goes our double engine down the stream of life . . . Cupid has fastened his shaft into my crankwheel, and matrimony shall be the connecting rod that sets us in motion."

In 1846, W. E. Aytoun recorded in *Blackwood's Magazine* that in theatres on the Surrey side "the nautical drama still flourishes in all its pristine force. The old British tar, in ringlets, pumps, and oilskin castor, still hitches up his trousers with appropriate oath . . . swims to the shore across a tempestuous sea of canvas with a pistol in each hand and a cutlass in his teeth, from the wreck of the foundering frigate; and sets foot once more on the British soil just in time to deliver Pretty Poll of Portsmouth, his

---

[1] *The English Fleet in 1342* by Thomas Dibdin.
[2] *The Dream Spectre* by T. E. Wilks.

affianced bride . . . from the persecutions of that bebuttoned pirate with the whiskers . . . and whose fall, after a terrific combat with basket-hilts and shower of fiery sparkles, brings down the curtain at the close of the third act amidst roars of unmitigated joy."

Eight years later, in 1854, the hero of *Ben Bolt*, by J. B. Johnstone, was still making remarks like "our heart's grappled 'ere one strain upon love's cable was known to us"—but now, at last, the idiom is losing its spirit. Before long it is in a rapid decline, hastened by the glorious uprising of the sailor of burlesque.

It is impossible to track a joke of this kind to any one originator, but I think the burlesque sailor certainly began outside the theatre. Smollett's salt sea characters had been carried on by such successful writers as Captain Marryat and Fenimore Cooper, and Marryat and Cooper had had a great many too many imitators. The burlesque sailor was first created as a skit upon the many saucy sailor boys in the early 19th century adventure novels.

Four years before his reference in *Blackwood's* to the nautical drama, Aytoun had composed an agreeable tale of the sea called *The Flying Dutchman* (1842). The scene is "the midst of the storm-tossed Atlantic" as "a heavy simoon, blowing N.E. by S. brought in the huge tropical billows mast-high from the Gulf of Labrador".

All the sails which usually decorated the majestic masts of H.M.S. Syncope (a real seventy-nine of the old Trafalgar build, teak built and copper-fastened) were reefed tightly up, with the exception of the mainsail, the spritsail, the mizzen-boom sail, and a few others of minor consequence. Everything was cleared away— halyards, hencoop, and binnacle had been taken down below, to prevent accidents; and the whole of the crew, along with the marines and boarders, piped to their hammocks. No-one remained upon deck except the steersman, as usual lashed to the helm; Josh Junk, the first bos'un; and the author of this narrative, who was then a midshipman on board the vessel, commanded by his uncle, Commodore Sir Peregrine Pendant.

"Skewer my timbers!" exclaimed Mr. Junk, staggering from one side of the ship deck to the other as an enormous wave struck us on the leeside, and very nearly unshipped the capstan—"Skewer my timbers, if this a'n't enough to put an admiral's pipe out! Why,

Master Tom, d'ye see,[1] its growing altogether more and more darkerer; and if it a'n't cleared by twelve bells, we'll be obligated to drop anchor, which a'n't by no means so pleasant, with a heavy swell like this, running at nineteen knots an hour in the middle of the wide Atlantic. How's her head, boy?"

"North by south it is, sir," replied the steersman.

"Keep her seven points more to the west, you lubber! Always get an offing when there's a wet sheet and a flowing sea. That's right, Jem! Hold her hard abaft. . . ."

This excellent jest is the first burlesque known to me of the jack tar of the novel. The jack tar of the stage was also burlesqued in a book long before he was burlesqued in the Theatre —by Dickens in his detailed description of the Crummles boys rehearsing a nautical combat at the inn on the Portsmouth Road (*Nicholas Nickleby*, 1838) and by Gilbert A'Beckett in one of his stage portraits in *George Cruikshank's Table Book* (1845).

When at sea, though only a common sailor, the stage tar is the most important personage in the vessel; and the captain frequently retires to the side of the ship—sitting probably on a water-barrel— in order to leave the entire deck at the service of the tar, while he indulges in a naval hornpipe. The dramatic seaman usually wears patent leather pumps and silk stockings, when on active service, and if we are to believe what he says, he is in the habit of sitting most un-necessarily on the main topgallant in a storm at midnight, for the purpose of thinking of Polly. When he fights he seldom condescends to engage less than three at a time. . . . The stage-tar sometimes carries papers in his bosom, which, as he can not read, he does not know the purport of; and though he has treasured them up, he has never thought it worth while to get anybody to look at them, but he generally pulls them out in the very nick of time, in the presence of some old nobleman, who glances at them, and exclaims, "My long-lost son!" at the same time expanding his arms for the tar to rush into. Sometimes he carries a miniature, and finds in some titled dame a mother to match it, or pulls up the sleeve of his jacket and shows a stain of port-wine upon his arm, which establishes his right to some very extensive estates, and convicts a conscience-stricken steward of a long train of villainies. At the close of his exploits it is customary to bring in the union-jack (nobody

---

[1] "D'ye see" is a sailorism much used by the original nautical characters of Smollett.

knows why it is introduced or where it comes from) and to wave it over his head, to the air of "Rule Britannia".

In that last sentence A'Beckett suggested a burlesque joke which Gilbert was to use, long afterwards, in *H.M.S. Pinafore* and again in *Ruddigore*.[1]

Thackeray's skit on Fenimore Cooper in *Novels by Eminent Hands* (1847) was written two years later than A'Beckett's sketch, and five years later that Aytoun's. "'There was a woman in our aft scuppers', says Tom Coxswain (an American sailor), 'when I went a-whalin in the little "Grampus" and Lord love you, Pumpo, you poor land-swab, she *was* as pretty a craft as ever dowsed a tarpauling. . . .' As he spoke, the hardy tar dashed a drop of brine from his tawny cheek, and once more betook himself to splice the taffrail."

In 1851, in the brief skit, *The Orphan of Pimlico* by Miss M. T. Wigglesworth, "many years Governess in the Nobility's families, and authoress of 'Posies of Poesy' 'Thoughts on the use of the Globe' etc.", Thackeray produced an Admiral the Hon. Hugh Fitzmarlinspike, complete with wooden leg and a flagship called *The Rumbustical*. Jack Marlinspike had been the name of an ordinary sailor character in *Roderick Random*. Here—assisted by the Fitz and other trimmings—the name has blossomed into a burlesque tradition.

The jolly jack tar joke reached the theatre in the general reaction against the extravaganza. *The Port Admiral* by Thomas Gibson Bowles (1863)—one of the Lacy "Sensation series"—is a full burlesque both of the saucy sailor and of the melodrama in which he was so conspicuous a figure.

> Farewell! Farewell to glory!
> Farewell the main and mizen truck, farewell
> My own gaff-topsail halyards—farewell sheets
> So often in the wind. Farewell main-brace
> That I so oft have spliced.

In these lines, which are not unlike Fielding's verse in *The*

---

[1] *George Cruikshank's Table Book* contains further marine burlesque in "Notes taken during the Late War in China by Captain Cutaway, of Her Majesty's Horse Marines". On board *The Shrimp*, "My gallant fellows mounted guard every day on the binnacle", says Captain Cutaway. He himself "used to sit for hours on the top of the compass (which remained boxed during the time we remained at anchor)".

Covent Garden Tragedy, the true voice of burlesque is heard again. Next, Jack Shivertimbers appeared in 1864 in *The Tyrant! The Slave!! The Victim!!! and The Tar!!!!*; and in 1866 Burnand scored an enormous success with his full length burlesque of *Black-Eyed Susan*, in which Miss Rosina Ranoe appeared as William, "with a dashing vivacity totally distinct from that which is generally displayed by the actresses of burlesque gentlemen".

> Shiver my anchors! bless my marlin-spikes!
> If this ain't just the sort o' thing I likes!
> Messmates, what cheer? (*They cheer.*)
>   Another! (*They cheer again.*)
>   Reef my spars!
> Naval and milit'ry: *sailors* with *Huzzas*.

The rhymes and the puns of extravaganza are still there. But Burnand was a wit: the burlesque cuts through the facetiousness: critical laughter is created: the burlesque sailor has plainly arrived. And, indeed, that something unusual had taken place in the theatre was clearly indicated in the press reports. "An unhackneyed subject", wrote *The Glowworm*: "A novel subject", said the *News of the World*. And the *Times* summed the good news up correctly when it wrote: "Mr. F. C. Burnand has made an excellent move by quitting the region of classical antiquity and turning into a new direction. . . . People were getting a little tired of those fabulous gods and goddesses. . . . But by taking *Black-Eyed Susan* for his theme Mr. Burnand has broken up entirely fresh ground. . . ."

Dickens, Aytoun, A'Beckett, Thackeray and Burnand created the jolly jack tar joke. Gilbert was to promote its apotheosis in *H.M.S. Pinafore*.

J. R. PLANCHÉ

THE first half of the 19th century was chiefly remarkable in the theatre for the triumphant development of the English melodrama, the popularity of which soon placed it beyond the fire of critical laughter. Skits of successful plays were produced from time to time, but hardly anything with a barbed wit. Dibdin's *Bonifacio and Bridgetina* [1] stands almost alone as a

---

[1] See pp. 88–90.

tolerable burlesque of melodrama. It is important because it was contemporary criticism. The far more famous *Bombastes Furioso* (1810) by W. B. Rhodes, G. Daniel's *Dr. Bolus* (1818) and J. R. Planché's first play *Amoroso, King of Little Britain* (1818) were all burlesques of a heroic tragedy which no longer existed. For all the effect that they had on these entertainments, Sheridan, Frere, Canning and Dibdin might never have enlarged the burlesque tradition at all. Here were the long names, the couplet, the well-loved simile—all the paraphernalia of mock tragedy—but the joke had no longer any contemporary application, and it was executed in undisguised imitation of earlier masterpieces.

> So when two feasts, whereat there's nought to pay
> Fall unpropitious on the self-same day,
> The anxious Cit each invitation views,
> And ponders which to take or which refuse:
> From *this* or *that* to keep away is loth,
> And sighs to think he can not dine at both.
>
> (*Bombastes Furioso*)

It is a good simile, but palpably derived, and presumably with veneration, from a famous passage in *Tom Thumb*.[1] In the 20th century people still laugh at the village maiden, the mortgaged farm, the jolly sailor and the wicked squire, though the melodrama, in which they flourished, has been long dead. The early 19th century accepted an antique prescription for laughter for the same reasons; they were attached to a joke, which had been kept artificially alive by the continued popularity of the operatic version of *Tom Thumb*. Even as late as 1872 one Charles S. Cheltnam produced a play called *Leatherlungos the Great* with long names and rhymed couplets in the *Tom Thumb* and *Chrononhotonthologos* tradition.

Humorists of the Regency period were satisfied to share a joke with the 18th century. Their successors were content to take a step even further backwards. Instead of shooting at the follies of contemporary drama, they returned to that ancient facetiousness, that original of burlesque laughter, the travesty.

James Robinson Planché was mainly responsible for the growth and popularity of 19th century extravaganza. But the

[1] See p. 35.

new entertainment had its roots deep in the past. Charles Dibdin's *Poor Vulcan* (1778), written mostly in the original octosyllabic burlesque couplet, is a piece of robust facetiousness about gods and goddesses, curiously like an early Planché extravaganza. So is *The Court of Alexander* by G. A. Stevens (1770), and, earlier again, Kane O'Hara's famous burletta, *Midas* (1762). Thomas Dibdin's *Don Giovanni* (1817)—written before Planché had had anything produced at all—is fully in the extravaganza form, and indeed includes the very word in its long comic descriptive title.

Extravaganza is not burlesque as Buckingham, Fielding, Sheridan and Canning understood the art. It is burlesque without an object, burlesque weakened into farce, a whimsical entertainment conducted in rhymed couplets or blank verse, garnished with puns, and normally concerned with classical heroes, gods and goddesses, kings and queens. The central idea might be a burlesque one: the interpolated songs might be parodies: but as a whole the extravaganza was pure travesty. It had no critical purpose. It was not aimed at any dramatic absurdity of the contemporary stage. The only burlesque element was the wide contrast between style and subject.

JUPITER: It's your deal Neptune—cut the cards, you Plutus.
Now, Neppy—turn up something that will suit us.
(*Olympic Revels* by J. R. Planché and
Charles Dance 1831.)

This is the old 17th century joke of Scarron and Charles Cotton re-created.

GHOST: I am the ombre of the King of Hearts.
QUEEN OF
  HEARTS: My husband!
KNAVE OF
  HEARTS: My late King!
KING OF
  SPADES: Avaunt and quit my sight—let the earth hide thee!
There is no speculation in those eyes
That thou dost glare withal!
GHOST: I do not play
At speculation.
KNAVE OF
  SPADES: No: he plays at fright.

KING OF

SPADES: What game is now afoot?

GHOST: Whist! Whist! oh Whist!

This sustained card language from Planché's *High, Low, Jack and the Game* (1833) shows the skill which he could bring to this form of writing. But it is an example of dexterity, not of burlesque. Later and lesser writers were to become so involved in the exercise of punning that they obliged themselves to resort not only to italics but even to explanations.

I've said *tonight* (*postman's knock heard*)

Two Knocks (nox)

That sort of thing (from H. J. Byron's *Babes in the Wood*, 1859) has nothing to do with the critical laughter of burlesque.

Planché's production of *Riquet with the Tuft* in 1836 was described by the author as "a turning point in the history of extravaganza". From then onwards he re-wrote the old fairy stories in plays full of charm, humour, and gaiety, greatly important in the history of the theatre as the originals of the modern kind of pantomime. These pieces lent themselves to burlesque performance: they contained parody—for instance Lord Factotum's song in *The Sleeping Beauty in the Wood* (1840) :

Verily! Verily!—Few could live now

Under the honours beneath which I bow—

but they were not burlesques. They were, indeed, what they called themselves, extravaganzas, and it would not be necessary to consider them here at all if it were not for the overwhelming influence which they had upon works which did claim to be burlesque.

An examination of 19th century burlesque, so named, discovers an extraordinary preponderance of classical or historical titles—burlesques upon the stories of Joan of Arc, Guy Fawkes, Penelope, Venus and Adonis, Helen of Troy, Hercules, Sardanapalus, Medea, Cupid and Psyche, Alcestis, Theseus and Ariadne, Fair Rosamund: or direct travesties of old plays like *Richard III*, *Hamlet*, *Othello* and *The Merchant of Venice*. There were also burlesques of contemporary productions, like *The Lady of Lyons* and *Der Freischutz*, but the majority of Victorian so-called burlesques, particularly in the early and middle part of the reign, were not connected with their own period. They

re-told old romances extravagantly and absurdly, in exactly
the same spirit as Scarron had retold the stories of antiquity.
They were not criticising the text, or laughing at the story
itself. The Victorian burlesque was an exercise in flippancy.

MACBETH: What mean these salutations, noble Thane?
BANQUO: These showers of *'hail'* anticipate your *reign*.

> (*Macbeth Travestie* by Francis Talfourd 1850.)

Even the title had to bear its part. *Shylock or The Merchant of
Venice Preserved, a Jerusalem Hearty-Joke* is Talfourd's *pièce de
résistance* for 1853.

This conception of burlesque was made abundantly plain in
a trifling sketch by Joseph Sterling Coyne called *Buckstone at
Home, or the Manager and his Friends* (1863). It is one of those
port-mortems on the Drama with Hamlet, Harlequin, Opera
etc. as characters. Towards the end Burlesque comes in—"that
graceless girl", as a character of high comedy calls her, and Sir
Peter Teazle declares himself disgusted that Fun's rusty toma-
hawk should be ousting Wit's polished rapier. Burlesque brings
with her a parade of burlesque characters—and lo! they are
all from Planché and Henry J. Byron and Brough—Cinderella,
Blue-Beard, Fortunio, Medea. Nothing could be clearer. For
the mid-Victorians the great characters of burlesque—Bayes
and Drawcansir, Aldiborontiphoscophornio, Lord Grizzle,
Huncamunca and Tilburina, had ceased to exist. The word had
already lost caste, and was on its way towards that debased
meaning which it now bears in the U.S.A., where 'Burlesque'
is a cheap variety show with a strip-tease artist as an essential
and principal ingredient.

The inclusion of Planché's characters in *Buckstone at Home*
was unfair. Planché had an exact understanding of the difference between extravaganza and burlesque, and ten years
earlier, in *The Camp at the Olympic*, he had written lines for "The
Spirit of Burlesque" which rebuked the immoderate facetiousness of his contemporaries.

> When in his words he has not one to the wise,
> When his fool's bolt *spares* folly as it flies;
> When in his chaff there's not a grain to seize on,
> When in his rhyme there's not a ray of reason;
> His slang, but slang—no point beyond the pun—
> Burlesque may walk, for he will cease to run.

And two years before *Buckstone at Home* he had written in "Temple Bar" in 1861: "If some have lavished a wealth of wit to which I could never pretend upon inferior structures, or suffered their racy spirits to ride rough-shod over the vulgar tongue, and plunge themselves into jungles of jingles and sloughs of slang, all I demand is not to be accused of having set the example".[1]

The 19th-century misuse of the word 'burlesque' is equally well illustrated by a sentence in the recently published criticisms of Charles Rice.[2]   Rice praises a travesty of *Douglas* by Leman Rede (March 11, 1837) by saying that it "stands second to nothing of its sort, save Dowling's *Othello, by Act of Parliament,* [1834], which is unquestionably the best burlesque that has ever appeared". Rice was no fool, and one can only suppose that the word 'burlesque' had lost its meaning. Presumably he would have classed *The Critic* as a play, and *Tom Thumb* as a burletta. To him a burlesque meant a travesty—and certainly *Othello, by Act of Parliament* is nothing more.

James Robinson Planché wrote or collaborated in 176 theatrical productions. Many of them afforded opportunities for burlesque acting. Very few were truly pieces of burlesque writing. *The Golden Fleece* (1845) was produced as a comment upon a performance of *Antigone* "after the Greek manner, on a raised stage, and with a chorus, which with Mendelssohn's music and Miss Vandenhoff's declamation, had made some sensation at Covent Garden".[3] Charles Mathews played the Chorus and it must have been a memorable performance, for twenty-five years later Percy FitzGerald was writing in his *Principles of Comedy* (1870) "Few play-goers will forget Charles Mathews in his representation of that odd portion of the Greek dramatis personae, the Chorus—that tedious body of moralisers and incessant interrupters of the business, who have perplexed and wearied so many a schoolboy with their Jeremiads and explanations."

The Golden Fleece was burlesque and there were burlesque

---

[1] As early as 1845 Planché had been accused of all these things by W. E. Aytoun, in a very sharp article against extravaganza in *Blackwood's Magazine*.

[2] *The London Theatre In The Eighteen-Thirties* by Charles Rice, edited by Arthur Colby Sprague and Bertram Shuttleworth (1950), p. 31.

[3] See J. R. Planché, *Recollections and Reflections* (1872), p. 293.

elements in many other of Planché's pieces. But he was not principally a writer of burlesque. He was the distinguished purveyor of his own dramatic form—derived in part from the French theatre, in part from English farcical writers of the 18th century. The comic writers who followed Planché's lead, plunged into the wildest jocosities and quickly promoted what Planché sadly described in his *Recollections* as "the rage for mere absurdity which my extravaganzas so unintentionally and unhappily gave rise to".[1] It was not to be expected that these writers should add anything to the burlesque tradition. Almost their only lasting influence derives from their pleasure in whimsical names and titles. Fielding (deriving from Swift), and Carey, had specialized in outlandish names like Huncamunca and Chrononhotonthologos. Planché substituted something more obviously comical in names like Perivigulus the Proud and Gander the Stupendous. All the extravaganza writers followed his example, and Thackeray (whose burlesque was in many ways influenced by the extravaganza school) improved the joke in *A Legend of the Rhine* (1845) by giving it a ghastly ring of authenticity: "Rowski, Prince of Donnerblitz, Margrave of Eulenschreckenstein, Count of Krötenwald, Schnauzestadt, and Golgenhügel, Hereditary Grand Corkscrew of the Holy Roman Empire"—which is the unremembered origin, no doubt, of Stephen Leacock's Guido the Gimlet of Ghent, and his friends Carlo the Corkscrew and Beowulf the Bradawl. The pleasantry still enlivens the programme of the Christmas pantomimes.

One benefit, which the burlesque tradition certainly owes to Planché, is a more temperate habit of playing. That burlesque was consistently over-played in the early 19th century is certain. At the end of the recognition scene in *The Critic* Sheridan wrote one word in the stage direction—"faints".

LADY: O wonderful event! (*faints*)[2]

The direction is what one would expect for a burlesque of Lady Randolph in *Douglas*. But in that collection of "the most approved Tragedies, Comedies, Operas and Farces" published

[1] Cf. Percy FitzGerald's denunciation two years before in *Principles of Comedy* (1870) p. 152, "The wretched stuff that is now palmed off as burlesque".
[2] The whole scene is printed on p. 52.

in 1824 under the title of *The British Drama*, the stage direction
is printed "They faint alternately in each other's arms." Anyone who knows what comedians will do for a laugh will easily
perceive what has happened. In forty-five years of acting the
"business" has been developed beyond the merit of the original
joke.

Another evidence is supplied by an agreeable anecdote told
by Genest of a performance of *Tom Thumb*.

Liston at first objected to playing Grizzle, and said he had determined never to play that part out of London—his reason was this
—one night when he acted Grizzle in some provincial theatre
T. P. Cooke, who was Glumdalca, had fastened a large bladder to
himself behind—when he died there was a loud explosion and
consequently incessant peals of laughter—this disconcerted Liston,
who of course could do nothing more with his part.

Planché, with the collaboration of Madame Vestris and
Charles Mathews, reformed both the playing and the dressing
of burlesque. Of *High, Low, Jack and the Game* he particularly
refers to the actors "not attempting to be *funny*, but acting it
as seriously as possible". And of *Olympic Revels* in 1831 he
writes of "the charm and novelty imparted to it by the elegance
and accuracy of the costumes, it having been previously the
practice to dress a burlesque in the most outré and ridiculous
fashion . . . Many old actors could never get over their early
impressions. Liston thought to the last that *Prometheus*, instead
of the Phrygian cap, tunic, and trousers, should have been
dressed like a great lubberly boy in a red jacket and nankeens,
with a pinafore all besmeared with lollipop!" [1]

The discipline of Planché and Madame Vestris, greatly
strengthened by Gilbert in his meticulous production of the
Savoy operas, has been a permanent gain to the English
theatre. A calculated gravity, and a solemn attention to correct
detail, is now recognized as essential to the conduct of burlesque.

W. S. GILBERT

W. S. GILBERT is an important figure in the history of English
burlesque: but he has been undeniably fortunate. His fame as

[1] *Recollections and Reflections*, p. 126.

the librettist of the Savoy operas has obscured the fact that he was also the author of dozens of other works of very small merit. He has been honoured with the name of satirist. He was not a satirist. His wit was strongly ironical, but it was a burlesque wit. He has been widely considered as the originator of an entirely new style of writing. He was not that either. At the beginning of his career he wrote so-called burlesques on popular successes, and, like all the other humorists, he wrote in rhymed couplets garnished with puns. He was an extravaganza writer, deriving, as they all did, directly from Planché. But whereas Henry J. Byron, the Broughs, and the A' Becketts were illegitimate descendants, denounced and denied by their parent, Gilbert was the acknowledged heir.[1]

"The rage for mere absurdity which my extravaganzas so unintentionally and unhappily gave rise to, has lasted longer than I anticipated," wrote Planché in 1872; "but there are unmistakable signs, I think, of its subsistence. As I remarked elsewhere, the writers of what is called 'the fast school' are killing themselves. 'They cannot live the pace—they must pull up, or break down and the wisest will yet win by a head'.[2] Mr. Gilbert is at present leading. He has come out of the ruck in gallant style, and is the first favourite with all the true lovers of the Drama."

That prophecy was written before the Savoy operas had even begun, while Gilbert was still writing farces in rhymed couplets like these from *La Vivandiere* (1867):—

LORD MARGATE: Declare yourself instanter, or I'll fell you! Your name?

ROBERTO (*disguised as* MANFRED): My name? Guess three times and I'll tell you.

MARQUESS OF
CRANBOURNE ALLEY: Hamlet?

LORD PENTONVILLE: The Stranger?

ROBERTO: No, that's two already.

LORD MARGATE: Robinson Crusoe?

ROBERTO: Pretty near—*Man freddy!*

---

[1] Planehé's Lord Factotum (Lord High Chamberlain, Lord High Steward, Lord High Constable, Lord High Treasurer, Great Grand Cup Bearer, Great Grand Carver) in *The Sleeping Beauty in the Wood* (1840) is clearly an ancestor of Gilbert's Pooh-Bah (1885).

[2] Planché is quoting himself from *Temple Bar*, November 1861. See p. 112.

LORD MARGATE: Oh, I remember—now I look again,
                 I saw you some time since at Drury Lane.
                                                    [*Yawning.*
ROBERTO: Yes: but so weakened by my sighs and yelps,
                 I couldn't "run"—e'en with the aid of (*P*)*helps.*

Gilbert remained an extravaganza writer all his days, but while those other humorists degraded the extravaganza into tittering farce, Gilbert elevated it into the realms of burlesque comedy. His importance lies in the fact that he tamed the ghastly high spirits of extravaganza, surrendered the puns, gave the couplets a well-earned rest, controlled (though he never entirely disdained) the facetiousness, rejected the travesty, and devoted his art, not to the eternal skitting of an old tale, but to the adornment of a new one.

Burlesque was a powerful ingredient in Gilbert's art. It did not dominate it. It comes out strongly in *Trial by Jury*, *H.M.S. Pinafore*, and *Ruddigore*; less strongly in *Iolanthe* and *The Pirates of Penzance*.[1] From the *Yeoman of the Guard* it is totally absent. *The Sorcerer* is farcical. Gilbert himself referred to "the burlesqueries of *Iolanthe* and *The Mikado*": but *The Mikado* and *The Gondoliers* are really ironical comedies. Pooh-Bah's memorable line, "Merely corroborative detail, intended to give artistic verisimilitude to an otherwise bald and unconvincing statement", is not a burlesque of anything. It is pure humour.

Princess Ida and *Patience* are the most acidulated of the operas, but—except perhaps for the character of Bunthorne—neither of them are punitive. They are comedies, highly salted with topical burlesque. Gilbert was not angry enough to be a satirist. It is impossible to feel that he had a righteous detestation for the Pre-Raphaelites or for higher education among women. Indeed, in the matter of *Princess Ida* Gilbert has left no room for argument. He called it "a respectful perversion" of Tennyson's *The Princess*. "I endeavoured so to treat it", he says, "as to absolve myself from a charge of wilful irreverence." He does not seem to have noticed that *Princess Ida* was also a sort of inversion of *Love's Labour's Lost*.

Patience and *Princess Ida* are enjoyed today as period pieces, not as living criticism. The burlesque has diminished, partly

[1] The 20th century, of course, misses the reference to the many early Victorian plays about pirates and wreckers on the Cornish coast.

because the objects are no longer topical, but chiefly because Gilbert's criticism was a criticism of behaviour rather than a criticism of literary style. The burlesque of rhymed couplets, similes, blank verse, stage directions, plagiarism, patriotism, villainy, is a criticism of style, and can be understood as long as writing endures. The burlesque of Burne-Jones attitudes and Oscar Wilde clothes, passes with the fashion, and the mockery of women's education is reduced to fantasy by its triumphant success.

Gilbert's contribution to the burlesque tradition rests on other achievements than *Patience* [1] and *Princess Ida*.

The work of Fielding, Jane Austen, Dickens, and Thackeray is powerful evidence of the fact that burlesque is nearly always written by young people. If Gilbert had written *Ruddigore* in 1877 he might have made that perfect criticism of melodrama which had been so long delayed. The *Ruddigore* of 1887 is disappointing. "The fishing village of Rederring in Cornwall" was an admirable programme joke, and sweet Rose Maybud (the adjective is her own) was a good heroine; [2] but Gilbert missed the real weaknesses of melodrama by being too clever about them, too topsy-turvy, too Gilbertian. *H.M.S. Pinafore*, nine years earlier, was not wholly a burlesque of melodrama, but it contained a number of melodramatic hits, more amusing and better conceived than anything in *Ruddigore*. Dick Deadeye, destined to villainy by the accident of name and face, has had a lasting influence on burlesque. The "dark secret" of Ralph Rackstraw's birth is an excellent joke and his address to Josephine a just criticism of the intolerable loquacity of melodrama heroes; but the greatest achievement in *H.M.S. Pinafore* is the burlesque of the jolly jack tar, a character belonging equally to melodrama and to comedy.

The jolly jack tar joke had been established years before

---

[1] It is worth noting, without emphasis, that the joke of the heroine determined to suffer rather than follow the dictates of the heart, had been made in *The Heroine* (1813), the full-length and very readable burlesque of the romantic novel, by Eaton Stannard Barrett. "Were there even some youth in the house", thinks the heroine, "who would conceive an unhappy attachment for me."

[2] The heroine of J. T. Haines' melodrama *My Poll and My Partner Joe* (1835) was called Mary Maybud. In the same play reference is made to an individual (who does not appear) called Dan Deadeye.

Gilbert brought it to the stage of the Opéra Comique in 1878. But no one before him had ever played the joke so well or on so large a scale. Besides, the particular version of it was his own, and was rooted in the much earlier *Bab Ballads*.

H.M.S Pinafore is a burlesque of the jolly jack tar theme from the moment the curtain rises, with the honest fellows singing,

> We sail the ocean blue
> And our saucy ship's a beauty;
> We're sober men and true,
> And attentive to our duty—

until that splendid moment when the crew acclaims Ralph Rackstraw with the cry,

> He is an Englishman!

The burlesque in the dialogue is equally discreet.

SIR JOSEPH: A British sailor is a splendid fellow, Captain Corcoran.
CAPTAIN: A splendid fellow indeed, Sir Joseph.
SIR JOSEPH: I hope you treat your crew kindly, Captain Corcoran.
CAPTAIN: Indeed I hope so, Sir Joseph.
SIR JOSEPH: Never forget that they are the bulwarks of England's greatness, Captain Corcoran.
CAPTAIN: So I have always considered them, Sir Joseph.

Ralph's exchange with Sir Joseph is an example of that joke of unexpected frankness now firmly established in the burlesque tradition.

SIR JOSEPH: You're a remarkably fine fellow.
RALPH: Yes, your honour.
SIR JOSEPH: And a first-rate seaman, I'll be bound.
RALPH: There's not a smarter topman in the Navy, your honour, though I say it who shouldn't.

Gilbert burlesqued the sailor again in Richard Dauntless in *Ruddigore*—but Richard is a bit overdone, and the joke here consists almost entirely in nautical jargon, not new enough to please until that moment when the fatuous Rose Maybud gets muddled up in it.

RICHARD: Belay, my lad, belay. You don't understand.
ROSE: Oh sir, belay, I beseech you.

Gilbert's second great contribution to the burlesque tradition is his brilliant use of operatic and general musical convention. Comic opera had come a long distance since *The Dragon of Wantley*. Dibdin and Bickerstaffe and Sheridan had moved away from burlesque to create a new convention for light comedy operetta: but the extravaganza writers had broken up that tradition by subjecting words and music to the disintegrating laughter of travesty. The importance of Gilbert's work as a librettist lies in the fact that he was not burlesquing, parodying, or travestying particular musical productions. He was burlesquing musical conventions in general.

It is often asserted that Gilbert was unmusical. He was only unmusical in the sense that he did not understand the practice of music. He could not write it or read it, but he understood, as well as any man ever did, the sort of words that music requires. He wrote his lyrics to musical rhythms, remembered or invented for his own secret purposes, and he was ready to alter the shape of a song to suit the particular requirements of Sullivan.

As Gilbert grew older, the burlesque of musical forms was reduced. In the later operas the songs are not more than the songs of first class operetta. But the earlier works—particularly *Trial by Jury* and *H.M.S. Pinafore*—are full of adroit burlesque. For instance, the exchange of compliments in recitative between Captain Corcoran and his crew—

CAPTAIN: My gallant crew, good morning.
ALL (*saluting*): Sir, good morning.
CAPTAIN: I hope you're all quite well.
ALL (*as before*): Quite well; and you, sir?
CAPTAIN: I am in reasonable health and happy
        To meet you all once more.
ALL (*as before*): You do us proud, sir!

Or the magnificently unsuitable words for the Barcarolle—

        Over the bright blue sea
        Comes Sir Joseph Porter, K.C.B.,

And the dramatic aria for Josephine,

        The hours creep on apace,
          My guilty heart is quaking!
        Oh, that I might retrace
          The step I'm taking.

Patience has a beautiful burlesque folk song,

> Prithee, pretty maiden—prithee tell me true
> (Hey, but I'm doleful, willow willow waly!)

Princess Ida has the Lady Blanche's noble contralto statement,

> Come, mighty Must!
> Inevitable Shall!

that curious mixture of comic song and stately measure,

> Sing, hoity, toity! Sorry for some!
> Sing, marry come up and my day will come!

and the admirable fatuity of

> Merrily ring the luncheon bell!
> Here in meadow of asphodel . . .

As many more examples might be given of Gilbert's uncommon skill in devising lyric shapes for music, apart from any burlesque purpose.

Gilbert's "Gilbertianism" was really the inheritance of his extravaganza training, the residue of a facetiousness that was never completely strained away. True burlesque needs a direct and simple approach, and Gilbert's way was altogether too circuitous. His manner gave him his character, but it stood in his way as a burlesque writer, and in *Ruddigore* it seriously damaged an excellent idea. Even so, his contribution to the burlesque tradition is great. *H.M.S. Pinafore* is a classic of burlesque, both for its treatment of the sailor joke and for its amiable abuse of operatic convention.

BERNARD SHAW

A T the turn of the 19th century George Bernard Shaw decided to protect the dramatic rights of his novel, *Cashel Byron's Profession* (1882) by writing, printing, and producing upon the stage, a dramatized version called *The Admirable Bashville* (published 1901, performed 1903) ; and because he was in a hurry (so he declared) he wrote it in blank verse, modelled on

"the melodious sing-song", "the pleasant-sounding rigmarole"
of the early Shakespeare and the pre-Shakespearean dramatists.

That was his first purpose—but at the end of the preface he
reveals a second one, in a submission to the reader remarkably
similar to the Beggar's bland recommendation at the beginning
of Gay's opera.[1]

> I have strictly observed the established laws of stage popularity
> and probability. I have simplified the character of the heroine, and
> summed up her sweetness in the one sacred word: Love. I have given
> consistency to the heroism of Cashel. I have paid to Morality, in the
> final scene, the tribute of poetic justice. I have restored to Patriotism
> its usual place on the stage, and gracefully acknowledged The
> Throne as the fountain of social honor. I have paid particular
> attention to the construction of the play, which will be found equal
> in this respect to the best contemporary models.
>
> And I trust the result will be found satisfactory.

The result is supremely satisfactory. Burlesque had grown out
of date in the English theatre, but a wit is sometimes con-
strained to write burlesque simply for the pleasure of it. Shaw's
burlesque was not directed against anything except his own
novel. There are no ghosts or similes or tragedy oaths in *The
Admirable Bashville*, no jibes at dramatic convention or stage
directions. The play is built upon two only of the accepted
jokes: it is a burlesque of Elizabethan blank verse, and it is
delicately woven with occasional plagiarisms. Earlier burlesques of blank verse had usually been extravagant—extravagantly flat, or flowery, or bombastic. Shaw's verse is big, full-
blooded stuff, very nearly good, and the plagiarisms are
proudly borrowed as though full worthy of inclusion in such a
work.

In writing the love story of a prize-fighter in Elizabethan
verse, Shaw returned to that earliest idea of burlesque—the
joke of contrast. In forcing a stately and archaic verse to
accommodate a modern and unrewarding theme, he was
making exactly the same joke as Fielding had made in describing a vulgar brawl in language suited to an Homeric combat.
The vehicle is too fine for the passenger, the words too big for
the sentiment.

[1] See p. 50.

> Ensanguined swine, whelped by a doggish dam,
> Is this thy park, that thou, with voice obscene,
> Fillst it with yodeled yells, and screamst my name
> For all the world to know that Cashel Byron
> Is training here for combat.

The language of the ring will not go quietly into blank verse, and there's the pleasure of it.

> Like all women, Lydia,
> You have the courage of immunity.
> To strike you were against his code of honor;
> But me, above the belt, he may perform on
> T' th' height of his profession. Also Bashville.

William Archer said that *The Admirable Bashville* was the best burlesque of rhetorical drama in English, but he was ill-advised to add that *Tom Thumb* and *Chrononhotonthologos* were not in the running with it. The rhymed couplets and the solemn sentiments of the heroic drama were something totally different from the rollicking verse of the 16th century. Fielding and Carey were not making the same joke. A wiser comparison might have been made between *The Admirable Bashville* and *The Covent Garden Tragedy* [1] for in that Augustan burlesque Fielding created a blank verse joke very similar to Shaw's. The comparison would not be to Fielding's disadvantage. It is enough to say that both burlesques are masterpieces.

The Admirable Bashville owes very little to its predecessors. Plagiarism was the only joke which Shaw accepted from the burlesque tradition. The only joke which he bequeathed to it was his variation of the blank verse joke. Buckingham, Fielding and Sheridan had burlesqued the verse of the 17th and 18th centuries. Shaw went back to the 16th century, and started a joke which Max Beerbohm was to develop into a general burlesque of the Elizabethan play.

STEPHEN LEACOCK

STEPHEN LEACOCK—like Gilbert—had an irritating weakness for repeating himself. But whereas Gilbert evidently cherished certain jokes, Leacock seems to have repeated himself

[1] See pp. 58–60.

because he couldn't bother to remember what he had said last. Out they all come, the old and the new, the trash and the wit, like a sieve full of pebbles and mud and nuggets of gold. Leacock wrote carelessly and too much, but his place in the tradition of English burlesque is assured by a wit peculiar to himself; by his development of the general burlesque; by his late in the day but subtle treatment of the sensational novel in *Winsome Winnie*; by his sustained burlesque of the problem play in *Behind the Beyond*; and by his meticulous burlesque of the melodrama in *Cast up by the Sea*.

With his first book (1910) Leacock introduced a new flavour into the burlesque of fiction. The early burlesques of the novel had all been written at length—some at inordinate length: E. S. Barrett's burlesque, *The Heroine*, was quite as long as the stories it criticized. The first to experiment with the potted novel, the short concentrated burlesque, was the American, Edgar Allan Poe, between 1831 and 1835; but Poe's burlesques did not sell and were only published after he had re-arranged them as serious stories.[1] It was not, therefore, under his influence that William Edmonstoune Aytoun and Theodore Martin (collaborators in the *Bon Gaultier Ballads*) wrote their short burlesques soon afterwards. Aytoun's burlesques of Captain Marryat [2] and Disraeli both date from 1842. Thackeray's more famous *Novels by Eminent Hands* followed in 1847. The joke was developed by Bret Harte, Francis Burnand, and a tribe of Victorians, and handed down, in the 20th century, to such successful practitioners as Owen Seaman and E. V. Knox.

The potted burlesque has usually been directed against novels by famous writers. Leacock devoted his attentions not to particular authors, but to styles of writing. His best subjects were taken from old stories in boys' magazines and penny novelettes, from romances about Earls and Countesses, tragedies at the old American homestead, and terrible adventures at sea. The *Nonsense Novels* of Stephen Leacock are essentially not by eminent hands, and it was this emancipation from direct parody, which enabled him to develop the joke of straightfaced nonsense, adumbrated by earlier writers, but never before executed with the skill and consistency which Leacock now brought to it.

[1] See *The Novel in Motley*, pp. 201–3.
[2] See p. 104.

"Lord Ronald . . . flung himself from the room, flung himself upon his horse and rode madly off in all directions." That sentence from *Gertrude the Governess* is the best known Leacockism. The trick consists in presenting a nonsensical statement with such gravity that it appears to be wholly reasonable. This, from *Who D'you Think Did It?*, is another eminent example of the art:

"Mr. Kelly," said Throgton thoughtfully, "the logic of your story is wonderful. It exceeds anything in its line that I have seen published for months. But there is just one point that I fail to grasp. The two bullet holes?"

"They were old ones," answered the sailor quietly. "My uncle in his youth had led a wild life in the west; he was full of them."

Except for the ancient joke of academic jargon, pure nonsense is a 19th century contribution to the burlesque tradition. "Motionless with terror, she rode on quicker than possible, while I followed at a still greater speed." That sentence, which might well have been written by Leacock, appeared in 1887 in *The Skull Hunters*, a burlesque by Walter Parke of *The Scalp Hunters* by Captain Mayne Reid. Nonsense had certainly established itself in English burlesque long before *Nonsense Novels*; the joke was an inheritance; but it was Leacock who groomed it, who cut out the accompanying chuckles, and served it up with a straight face.

At its best the Leacockism is something better than nonsense. It is nonsense with a hidden truth in the middle of it. In *Caroline's Christmas*, for instance, the occupation of Anna, the farmer's wife, is plainly nonsensical—but once you have been shocked into accepting that occupation as reasonable, the Leacockism becomes a literary judgment.

Anna, with the patient resignation of her sex, sat silent, or at times endeavoured to read. She had taken down from the little wall-shelf . . . *Holy Living and Holy Dying*. She tried to read it. She could not. Then she had taken Dante's *Inferno*. She could not read it. Then she had selected Kant's *Critique of Pure Reason*. But she could not read it either.

This from "*Q*" is an equally sound criticism of the credulous.

"Do you believe in the supernatural?" he asked.
I started as if I had been struck.

At the moment when Annerly spoke of the supernatural I had been thinking of something entirely different. The fact that he should speak of it at the very instant when I was thinking of something else, struck me as at least a very singular coincidence.

In his early works Leacock was able to vary this jest again and again. *Sunshine Sketches of a Little Town* (1912), his third and best book, is not a burlesque. It is an ironic comedy, a Canadian parallel to *Our Village*. It is not a burlesque—but burlesque seeps into it, and with it comes the peculiar Leacock device for laughter.

"I am old now, gentlemen," Bagshaw said, "and the time must soon come when I must not only leave politics, but must take my way towards that goal from which no traveller returns."

There was a deep hush when Bagshaw said this. It was understood to imply that he thought of going to the United States.

Arcadian Adventures with the Idle Rich (1915), which is a near-satire, is equally adorned by this extraordinary trick, this quick left and right, which first stops the reader with a jolt, and then hits him in the mind.

The Grand Opera had sung itself into a huge deficit and closed . . . though the fact that the deficit was nearly twice as large as it had been the year before showed that public interest in music was increasing.

The roots of Leacock's humour can be traced, returning through the 19th century, to Mark Twain, Artemus Ward, and Bret Harte, to Gilbert A'Beckett, Thackeray and Planché, to the beginnings of the romantic and melodramatic theatre, to the fathers of modern burlesque, Frere and Canning. Some of the things that Leacock laughs at—the protestations of the virtuous, the malice of the wicked, the self-criticism, abnegation, and gentle goodness of the repentant, are well known characteristics of Kotzebue and the early Schiller and Goethe. Leacock may never have read the German dramatists. He laughs, never the less, at an English way of writing which is inherited from them.

Stephen Leacock wrote nothing directly for the stage, and he would have no place in this book if it were not for the fact that he was as deeply amused as Dickens had been by the absurdities of the theatre, and that, like Dickens, he wrote burlesques of the drama in the form of descriptions. *Behind the Beyond* (1913) is almost a play as it stands; *Over the Footlights* (1923) is a collection of burlesque scenarios; many of the burlesque novels are dramatic in shape, and several have body enough to be adapted for the stage with little alteration.[1]

The principal item of *Over the Footlights* is that perfect burlesque of melodrama which the world had so long awaited. Many writers have giggled at melodrama, and many too many have laughed it out of countenance. But no writer, except Dickens, has ever treated it with anything like Leacock's gusto. And no writer of critical burlesque has ever treated the subject at such length. Dickens's summary of Mr. Vincent Crummles's production at the Portsmouth theatre runs to about a thousand words. *Cast up by the Sea* is a full ten thousand words, and is the most critically exact of all melodramatic burlesques.

"Everybody who has reached or passed middle age looks back with affection to that splendid old melodrama, *Cast up by the Sea*," he begins. "Perhaps it wasn't called exactly that. It may have been named *Called back from the Dead*, or *Broken up by the Wind*, or *Buried Alive in the Snow*, or anything of the sort. In fact, I believe it was played under about forty different names in fifty different forms. But it was always the same good old melodrama of the New England coast, with the farmhouse and the yellow fields running down to the sea, and the lighthouse right at the end of the farm, with the rocks and the sea beyond, looking for trouble." And from there he goes on to a detailed description of the plot and all the famous ingredients of the old melodrama. Here are the two hired men at the farm (cutting real wheat as the curtain rises) and Phoebe, the help, who has a comic love scene with Rube whenever the strain of the drama demands alleviation. Here is Farmer Haycroft and his lovely daughter, arriving in a buggy drawn by a real horse; and a freckled boy who "is in all the melodramas. It is his business to get his ears boxed, mislay the will, lose the mortgage, forget to post the letters, and otherwise mix up the plot." Here is the famous farmhouse supper party for the neighbours, and Martha, the farmer's wife, alternately making pancakes and groaning

---

[1] Basil Macdonald Hasting adapted "*Q*". The author of this book has adapted *Behind the Beyond*, *Winsome Winnie*, *The Split in the Cabinet*, and *Who d'you think did it?* (under the title of *The Billiards Room Mystery*).

"The sea, the sea! I see it all so bright and calm in the sunlight. But will it give me back my boy?" And here is the son—not drowned at all—returning to the old home in disguise and getting shot by his own father. And here is Lawyer Ellwood, and the mortgage, and the farmer's daughter marrying the lawyer's son and getting turned out into the stormy night.

Two years elapse after that—and then the scene is the sea shore, with the tempest rising and everyone saying "God help all poor souls out at sea." A wreck is seen in the dark distance, and then a boat that drifts towards the reef where the lighthouse stands. As the curtain falls, a flash of lightning shows the farmer's daughter kneeling in the bow, in an attitude of prayer.

In Act 4, the farmer's son—the one who was shot: he's recovered now—dives head first from the lighthouse tower to rescue his sister, while, with hoarse cries and jagged sentences, the assembled fishermen describe the conflict which is happening "off", till "with one glorious haul up comes the line from the roaring sea with Jack at the end of it, and fast held in his encircling arm, the fainting form of his sister . . . There is a cry of 'Saved! Saved!' and Hiram Haycroft, clasping the senseless form of his daughter to his heart, cries: 'My little gal! Cast up by the sea!' and down comes the curtain in a roar of applause."

And so to Act 5 and all the explanations, until Phoebe enters carrying the essential baby, and the farmer lets fly the final sentiment: "Ay, lads, pin your hope in Providence, and in the end you land safe in front."

Cast up by the Sea is a perfect example of the truth that the best burlesque is always directed against the objects of its affection. It is because he has loved the melodrama that Leacock has been so successful in burlesquing it; and, by some subtle infusion of sincerity, he has contrived, not only to amuse the reader, but even to attract his interest to the drama itself. There lingers in this burlesque some ancient power, left over from the 19th century, with skill to touch upon human emotions. We are almost betrayed as we turn the page and come unexpectedly on the farmer's wife sinking beside her wounded son. We feel a flutter in the throat as the fishermen cry "He's swimming to her! Hold fast the line there! He's got her!" And, all the way through, we are conscious of a genuine curiosity about the outcome of events, an honest anxiety for a happy issue from misfortune. Time was when *Cast up by the Sea* was a fine piece: there can be no doubt about that. It remains an extremely funny one.[1]

Winsome Winnie (1920) was a burlesque of the sensational novel. But its theme is melodramatic, it is shaped for the theatre, and in it Leacock has accumulated a mass of critical points which earlier humorists had missed. Lawyer Bonehead, for instance, is something new. He is also the supreme example of that joke of unexpected frankness, which had been used before, but never so well, by Thomas Dibdin and W. S. Gilbert.

Miss Winifred—you are this morning twenty-one, and my guardianship is at an end. I have therefore sent for you to render an account of my trust—to declare to you the disposition that has been made of your property . . . This first document refers to the sum of two thousand pounds left to you by your great uncle. It is lost. If you will give me your best attention, I will endeavour to tell you how I lost it.[2]

In one of the Lacy "sensation" plays, *Alice, The Mystery, or the Parentless Maiden of the Cottage on the Cliff* (1865) by John Smith, some humour had been made out of "the dark secret" surrounding the heroine's birth.

I am not thy father, nor never was thy father, or ever shall be.

Followed by—

ALICE: Ah, my mother! do not, in mercy's name, mention *her*—my mother!
ADAM: Alas, my Alice! She, my wife, was not your mother.

---

[1] Among many scoring shots in *Cast up by the Sea*, Leacock's hit at the comic countryman was particularly well aimed. He made Rube exactly the character described by Dickens in *Nicholas Nickleby*, exactly the character described by Gilbert A'Beckett in *George Cruikshank's Table Book*, where he remarks that the stage lady's maid "sometimes unites herself to a low-comic country man, whom she has been snubbing all through the piece, but who, when he has a chance of being accepted, looks like a great fool, and says, 'Well I doant noa, thou beest woundy pratty', which is at once clutched at as an offer of marriage". A'Beckett also wrote a sketch of the heroic countryman, another established figure of the melodrama, own brother to the jolly jack tar, and Cruikshank made an admirable picture of him with the village maiden on one side and the squire on the other.

[2] These quotations are from the dramatized version of *Winsome Winnie*.

This is weak stuff compared with a similar joke of Leacock's where the familiar mixture of gravity and nonsense produces something startlingly funny.

WINIFRED: Then—oh pardon my folly—I am but a poor inadequate girl—a mere child in business—but tell me, I pray, what is there left to me of the money that you have managed?

MR. BONEHEAD: Nothing, Miss Winifred, nothing at all. Everything is gone. And I regret to say that it is also my painful duty to convey to you a further disclosure of a distressing character. It concerns—your birth.

WINIFRED: Just heaven! Does it concern my father?

MR. BONEHEAD: It does, Miss Clair. . . . Your father was not your father.

WINIFRED: Oh sir—my poor mother! How she must have suffered!

MR. BONEHEAD: Miss Clair . . . Your mother was not your mother—

Gilbert had noticed the verbosity of heroes and heroines; Leacock, by keeping a straighter face, improved upon him.

Nay! Kneel not to me! If I have done aught to deserve the gratitude of one who, whoever she is, will remain for ever present as a bright memory in the breast of one in whose breast such memories are all too few, he is all too richly paid. If she does that, he is blessed indeed.

In a little known play, *A Sensation Novel* (published in 1912), Gilbert, long before Pirandello, had had the idea of allowing the characters of a novel to talk the story over. The smug heroine roundly states that she wishes the smug hero had not intervened to stay the hand of the far more attractive villain. Leacock works the same joke with admirable discretion in *Winsome Winnie*, when Lord Wynchgate ("one of the most contemptible of the greater nobility of Britain") and his friends, Lord Dogwood and the Marquis of Frogwater, arrive at Winifred's humble lodgings with the declared intention of abducting her. "Abducted!" murmurs Winifred, as she hastily fluffs out her hair, puts a touch of rouge on her cheeks and a little darkening on the eyebrows. "Abducted! And by three of them! Oh the horror of it! The shame . . ."

Burlesque has declined in the last hundred years. Partly, this

10

is due to the alteration in the theatrical bill. In the days when an audience expected a tragedy followed by songs and dances, and then a farce, there was room for burlesque. Now, when a single play suffices to fill an evening, the burlesque is crowded out—for good burlesque, like any tonic, should be short and strong, and except in the form of comic opera, it will not often make a complete entertainment.[1] Another powerful reason for the absence of burlesque from the English stage is the equal absence of any eccentric form of writing. The days of heroic tragedy and melodrama are over. Modern dramatists (except Fry and Eliot) have settled down to a period of thoroughly competent, and undistinguished work. We have no eccentricities to burlesque. Now and then a revue may contain a skit on a contemporary success, but that, like the Victorian extravaganza, is travesty for travesty's sake. Ibsen and Chekov have often been travestied, but they offer a very small target to critical burlesque. Burlesque is directed at follies. Ibsen and Chekov do not provide the necessary material.

One opportunity for adding to the burlesque tradition was provided by the problem play of the late 19th and early 20th century. The problem play was melodrama in the drawing-room. It was just as improbable as melodrama but much more polite. The distresses of the village maiden were transferred to a lady of London society. Instead of the village squire the trouble-raiser was a diplomat or a cabinet minister. If the hero were a sailor he would certainly be R.N., and commissioned.

In one thing the problem play differed from the melodrama. It was less moral. In the melodrama the story ended happily, and the heroine always succeeded in escaping a fate worse than death. In the problem play the heroine had usually fallen into trouble before the play began. That was the problem. And it wasn't always possible to get her out of it. This gave the dramatist magnificent opportunities. There could be denunciations,

[1] Probably the last full-length burlesques produced in London were the author's *Aladdin* (1931) and *The Pride of the Regiment*, written with Scobie Mackenzie (1932). Both works have music, in burlesque of theatrical convention, by Walter Leigh. Ivor Novello's burlesque of the Ruritanian Operetta in *Gay's the Word* (1951) must be mentioned, but it is not a full-length burlesque in itself. Terence Rattigan's splendid *Harlequinade* (1948) was not truly a piece of burlesque writing. It was a vehicle for burlesque acting—which is something different.

recriminations, selfless surrenders, forgivenesses, and remorse. It was all very tense, and very neatly put together, and everybody in the audience was made to feel that the problem was very nearly their own.

In *Behind the Beyond* Stephen Leacock wrote a remarkably well sustained burlesque of this Pinero-George Alexander kind of piece. It was not written exactly in dramatic form, but the three acts were described from start to finish, with dialogue, stage directions and comments, and it was an easy matter to arrange it for performance.

Sir John Trevor, M.P., is twenty-five years older than his wife Lady Cicely, and Lady Cicely is being "starved"—"all that she has," remarks Leacock, "is money, position, clothes, and jewelry. These things starve any woman. They cramp her. That's what makes problem plays."

At the beginning of the play Sir John is chattering away about politics. "An important sitting—the Ministers will bring down the papers—the Kafoonistan business. The House will probably divide in committee. Gatherson will ask a question. We must stop it at all costs. The fate of the party hangs on it."

Anyone can see that Lady Cicely is sick of politics. The fact is she is in love with Sir John's secretary, Jack Harding, and when Sir John comes suddenly upon the guilty pair, she denies nothing. "I love him," she says, "I'm not ashamed of it. What right have you to deny it me? You gave me nothing. You made me a chattel, a thing—you starved me here. You throttled me. You smothered me—I couldn't breathe. And now I am going, do you hear, going away, to life, to love, behind the beyond!"

Lady Cicely and Jack Harding depart. Sir John sinks into a chair. A valet enters with a cablegram. Sir John obligingly reads it aloud. "He is dead. My duty is ended. I am coming home—Margaret Harding."

Jack Harding? Margaret Harding? The audience perceives a delightful possibility; and the curtain falls.

Act two is in Paris, in the apartment where Jack and Lady Cicely are manifestly living together. Mrs. Harding turns up. So does Sir John. Lady Cicely (already afflicted by a consumptive cough) decides to renounce her love. Harding attacks Sir John with a knife and our best suspicions are confirmed as Mrs.

Harding casts herself between them, and entreats her son to refrain from murdering his father.

The third act takes place in Mrs. Harding's house and is largely composed of pregnant silences. Sir John has called to tell Mrs. Harding that Jack has sailed for Peru.

"He will do well in Peru," says Mrs. Harding. She is imitating a woman being very brave. . . .

Presently Mrs Harding speaks again in a low tone.

"You have other news, I know."

"I have other news."

"Of her?"

"Yes. I have been to Switzerland. I have seen the curé—a good man. He has told me all there is to tell. I found him at the hospice, busy with his *œuvre de bienfaisance*. He led me to her grave."

Sir John is bowed in deep silence.

Lady Cicely dead! Everyone in the theatre gasps.

Dead! But what an unfair way to kill her!

Nothing remains now except for Mrs. Harding and Sir John to solve their own problem. He says he is going to Kafoonistan. "There is a man's work to be done there. The tribes are ignorant, uncivilized." Mrs. Harding (and this is pure *Stella*) says she is going to return to Balla-Walla. "My life will be useful there. The women need me—I will teach them to read, to sew, to sing." Each tries to dissuade the other. Neither will give way. But it can't end like that, and after each has put up a good show of self-sacrifice, Sir John takes her hand.

"And you," he says, "you will think of me sometimes in Balla-Walla?"

"Yes, always. All day when I am with the Maharanee and her women, and at night—the great silent Indian night—when all the palace is asleep, and there is heard nothing but the sounds of the jungle, the cry of the hyena, and the bray of the laughing jackass, I shall seem to hear your voice. . . . I have heard it so for five-and-twenty years."

He has moved to her.

"Margaret!"

"John!"

"I cannot let you go—your life lies here—with me—next my heart—I want your help, your love, here inside the beyond."

Like everything produced by Stephen Leacock, *Behind the Beyond* is written light-heartedly and carelessly, as though he had no notion of its merits. In fact Leacock was the first man since Gilbert to add anything new to the tradition of English burlesque. The problem play was as good a target as the German translation had been. Leacock hit it smack in the gold.

MAX BEERBOHM

Savonarola Brown, perhaps the most entertaining theatrical burlesque ever written, was published in 1919, six years after *Behind the Beyond*. Like that play, and like *The Rovers*, *Savonarola* was not intended to be acted, and was not set out in a form immediately suited for the stage.[1] Unlike *The Rovers* and *Behind the Beyond*, its laughter was directed against almost nothing in the contemporary theatre. Canning and Frere attacked the German drama. Leacock attacked the problem play. Max Beerbohm presented a burlesque without a purpose. *Savonarola* is a tragedy, written in flat blank verse, woven with plagiarism —but it is not aimed at any Cumberland. It does not ape the style of any modern writer. It does not rebuke the extravagance of any modern school of writing. If it were not for the fact that it glances at the problem of producing period plays in a realistic manner, *Savonarola* might have been a burlesque of Elizabethan drama born out of due time—the burlesque which might have been written by some Jacobean wag, and was not.

In its general effect *Savonarola* is unique. Yet most of its characteristics derive from the main tradition. The heroine mad goes back via *Dr. Bolus*, *The Critic* and *The What D'ye Call It* to one of the early jokes of burlesque. The simile is in the direct line of descent from *The Rehearsal*. The blank verse and the rhymed ending returns to Sheridan and Fielding. The joke of plagiarism is inherited from Sheridan; the joke of stage directions from Frere and Canning.[2] *Savonarola* is a codification of the burlesque tradition, as *The Critic* had been a hundred and forty years earlier. But Beerbohm's own contribution to that tradition is

[1] But it did reach the stage in a production by Nigel Playfair at the Haymarket Theatre, in 1930.

[2] See p. 83.

not inconsiderable, and consists in at least four valuable additions: his own particular version of the blank verse joke, the burlesques of Elizabethan humour and Elizabethan song, and the burlesque of crowd scenes and production methods.

Thackeray had burlesqued the baronial jester in his continuation of *Ivanhoe*, *Rebecca and Rowena* (1846 and 1850). "There be buzzards in eagles' nests," darkly observes Wamba. "There be dead men alive, and live men dead. There be merry songs and dismal songs. Marry, and the merriest are the saddest sometimes. I will leave off motley and wear black, gossip Athelstane." The Shakespearean fool, much given to riddles and other curious gaieties, is a different creature from the jester of romance, and Beerbohm's burlesque is something much better than a repetition of Thackeray's joke. All the inscrutable japes of Elizabethan humour are comprehended in the encounter between Lucrezia and the Borgia's Fool.

LUCREZIA: How many crows may nest in a grocer's jerkin?
FOOL: A full dozen at cock-crow, and something less under the
         dog-star, by reason of the dew, which lies heavy on men
         taken by the scurvy.

And all the lyrics in the Shakespearean album are echoed in the Fool's song.

> Fly home, sweet self,
> Nothing's for weeping,
> Hemp was not made
> For lovers' keeping,
>   Lovers' keeping.
> Cheerly, cheerly, fly away.

The burlesque of the crowd scene is more elaborate, being at once a burlesque of the dramatic oration and of the producer who enlivens it with realistic action.

                              Citizens!

        [Prolonged yells and groans from the crowd.

Yes, I am he, I am that same Lorenzo
Whom you have nicknamed the Magnificent.

        *[Further terrific yells, shaking of fists, brandishings of bill-
        hooks, insistent cries of 'Death to Lorenzo'! 'Down with the*

*Magnificent!' Cobblers on fringe of crowd, down c. exhibit
especially all the symptoms of epilepsy, whooping-cough, and
other ailments.*

You love not me.

[*The crowd make an ugly rush.* LORENZO *appears likely to
be dragged down and torn limb from limb, but raises one
hand in the nick of time, and continues:*

Yet I deserve your love.

[*The yells are now variegated with dubious murmurs. A cob-
bler down* c. *thrusts his face feverishly in the face of another
and repeats, in a hoarse interrogative whisper 'Deserves our
love?'*

The scene in the Piazza at Florence is not much shorter than
Shakespeare's scene in the Forum at Rome; and it is a lot
funnier.

The largest of Beerbohm's four gifts to burlesque is his blank
verse. Fielding's joke consisted in the wonderful unsuitability
of his subject for verse of any description. The joy of Sheridan's
poetry lies in its flowery opulence. Bounding vitality is the
characteristic of Shaw's. Beerbohm, improving upon Buckingham, invented a verse of miraculous flatness, which can only
be defined as Iambic prose cut into ten-syllabled lines.

O my dear Mistress, there is one below
Demanding to have instant word of thee.
I told him that your Ladyship was not
At home. Vain perjury! He would not take
Nay for an answer.

The humour of *Savonarola Brown* is entirely delightful. But it
stands apart from the rest of theatrical burlesque. It has been
arranged for the stage, but it does not truly belong there. It is
a unique literary prank, but it is removed from the living theatre
by the fact that its criticism is not contemporary.

It was A. P. Herbert who brought the Elizabethan joke inside the playhouse, with his *Two Gentlemen of Soho* (1927).

PANTOMIME AND BALLET

IN the second half of the 19th century, and the first few years of
the 20th, burlesque was a principal feature of the English panto-

mime. In the course of the 18th century the pantomime had
developed from a set of dances to a unique conglomeration of
mime, ballet, acrobatics, farce, tricks, and song, increasingly
enlivened by that basic kind of burlesque laughter, the malicious
confusion of high and low. Scenes in the laundry, and the
kitchen were among the earliest jokes of pantomime. The pre-
cipitation of the wrong people into such scenes converted a
farcical joke into a burlesque one; but when the wrong people
became involved of their own free will, when the Queen began
to take a housewife's interest in the cooking, or a woman's
delight in ironing her consort's underwear, then a burlesque
joke was converted into one of the finest burlesque situations
ever enjoyed in the English theatre.

The joke was rooted in the past—plainly related both to the
classical travesties of Scarron and to that ancient licence of the
church for the occasional debasement of the mighty. But burlesque humour had undergone a refinement since the days of
Scarron, and the confusion of high and low no longer neces-
sitated a tittering denigration of the great. Had a Queen been
debased to the kitchen by Scarron, the laughter would have
been cruel; but the willing indulgence of a Queen in such
employment—because, from some quirk of majesty, she prefers
to play a housewife's part—is quite another matter. In such a
situation the secrets of a woman's heart may be unlocked. Certainly, in the hands of a fine artist like Dan Leno, a pantomime
dame has seemed to make a commentary upon life as just and
as valuable as anything to be found in serious drama.

Pantomime might have decayed and died in the middle of
the 19th century. Its tricks had grown familiar, and there were
no longer acrobatic artists sufficiently skilled to perform them.
Instead of dying, it was rejuvenated (and transformed in the
process from the ancient harlequinade to the form in which we
know it today) by the wit of the extravaganza writers, and in
particular by Planché and Henry J. Byron. Honour must
always be paid to Byron for his invention of Buttons (Buttoni
when he first appeared in 1860) Prince Pekoe, and above all
Widow Twankey (1861) a character, who, in the older spectacles of *Aladdin*, had never been more than an ordinary oriental
widow of the name of Mustapha. This intrusion into the Eastern
scene of a housewife obviously English was a refinement upon

the topsy-turvy joke of high and low. The Widow Twankey keeping her end up with the Emperor of China is as good a burlesque situation as that of the Queen at the pudding basin.

Other essentially burlesque features of the pantomime include an indecent indulgence in food, a joke which goes back, by way of Grimaldi, to the Italian actors of the *commedia dell' arte*; the devastating commentary upon human affairs contributed by the horse in *Cinderella* and *Aladdin*, the cow in *Jack and the Beanstalk*, and—to a lesser degree—the cat in *Dick Whittington*; and the rhymed couplets, ill-written in these days, but still retaining a link with Byron and Planché, Carey and Fielding, Gay and Buckingham.

It is a further example of a topsy-turvy world that the serious features in this naturally burlesque entertainment should have been the occasion of burlesque in others. As long ago as 1860— many years before Gilbert wrote *Iolanthe*—Henry J. Byron invented a slightly acidulated Fairy Queen, and, many times since then, the Fairy has been burlesqued in cabaret and revue. The chorus has been mocked also, but the figure who has chiefly attracted the burlesquer is that unique support of Pantomime, the principal boy, with her shapely legs and dashing manner, and her powerful gift for song.

Every pantomime contains a song in which the principal boy adjures the audience to be of good cheer. In her opinion the clouds will soon roll away, bringing blue skies and sunshine for everyone. Keep smiling, she tells us, and everything will be all right. She then slaps her thigh and reduces the house to a paroxysm of pleasure by executing a brisk marching manœuvre, supported by the chorus, attired in military uniforms largely composed of ostrich feathers. The devotion of so much efficiency to the propagation of a sentiment so jejune and so illogical, is irresistible. In the midst of a burlesque entertainment the thigh-slapper is itself a perfect target for burlesque criticism.

The dance was very early a part of the burlesque tradition. Anything so simple or so finnicking as folk dancing, anything so skilful or so graceful as ballet dancing, lays itself open to mischievous comparison. Possibly the bergomask performed by Quince and his friends was funny. Certainly there was a burlesque dance in *The Rehearsal*. In the season of 1781 George

Colman produced *Medea and Jason* at The Haymarket, a burlesque "of a grand serious ballet, then acting, with great applause, on the other side of the way, at the Italian Opera-House."[1] Grimaldi burlesqued the ballet at the beginning of the 19th century, and, a few years later, Dickens contributed a famous description of Miss Ninetta Crummles and Mr. Folair at the Portsmouth theatre. A burlesque of Mlle. Duvernay in the Cachoucha was danced by Tom Matthews in 1837, and the same turn is often included in modern pantomime. It is a joke of which variety artists, and indeed variety audiences, never tire.

Unfortunately, burlesque of the ballet is a jest which can only survive in the memory. Excepting that all too short account of "The Indian Savage and the Maiden", happily preserved in *Nicholas Nickleby*, there is no book of a burlesque ballet. And ninety-nine times in a hundred the music for a burlesque ballet is only borrowed from something extremely familiar. But there have been examples of original music written for the purpose: the late Walter Leigh composed some admirably foolish music for a Russian ballet, and a twinkling Fairy Ballet and a "Ballet of Jewels" for *Aladdin*; and Dennis Arundell has composed a fragment alleged to be from the original music of "The Indian Savage and the Maiden".

There is one other lasting evidence of ballet burlesque. From time to time, caricature has contributed to the tradition of humour, things, which, without its prompting, might only have been guessed at. Several pictures, for instance, were made by Gillray, at the end of the 18th century, as a comment, first, upon the scantiness of the ballet dancers' clothes, and, later, in strong satire upon the Bishop of Durham's denunciation of the dancers as people likely to destroy British morality and religion —for which express purpose (so he declared) they had certainly been sent as agents of a malevolent French Government. This absurdity (March 1798) inspired several cartoons, one of which shows the dancers performing "La Danse à L'Evêque", securely covered in front by episcopal aprons, but regrettably bare behind. More in the amiable tradition of burlesque is a cartoon published by Gillray in 1796 called "Modern Grace, or the Operatical Finale to the ballet Alonzo e caro" (1796). It depicts

[1] George Colman, *Random Records* (1830), Vol. 2, p. 58.

Mlle Rose, Didelot, and Mlle Parisot, principal dancers in the
ballet "Alonzo e Cora" which had just been produced at the
Opera House. The alteration in the title from "Cora" to "caro"
is Gillray's latin witticism on the nakedness of the ladies.

This entertaining picture attracted Rowlandson so much that
he made his own delightful version of it—full of laughter and
without malice towards anyone. And a few years later, in *The
Microcosm of London*, he copied the general grouping for the
ballet scene on the stage of the Opera House.

Didelot's most famous ballet, "Flore et Zephire", in which he
made use of wires to achieve aerial flight, was also produced in
London in 1796. Revived in Russia in 1801, in Paris in 1815,
in London in 1830, the vitality of this work may be judged by
a remark in *The Pickwick Papers*, Chapter XLI. "Bravo! Heel
over toe—cut and shuffle—" says one prisoner at the Fleet to
another, who is dancing the hornpipe—"pay away at it,
Zephyr! I'm smothered if the Opera House isn't your proper
hemisphere."

This ballet, and Taglioni's performance in it, was the object
of the burlesque pictures which Thackeray published in Paris
in 1836, in a pamphlet called *Flore et Zephyr* with descriptive
notes in French, signed Théophile Wagstaff. They prove a plain
continuity of laughter between the Flore et Zephyr of 1836 and
the Nervo et Knox of 1952.[1]

SUMMARY

IN the following summary I have assembled what seem to me
to be the chief ingredients of English theatrical burlesque. It
has not been my purpose to peer into the dark backward beyond
the Elizabethan drama—for while we can perceive, for instance,
that academic jargon, pomposity, lyrical effusions and dramatic
narrations were burlesqued by Aristophanes, there is no reason
to suppose that the English versions of such obvious jokes were
derived from that source. This list is merely a rough indication

[1] Thackeray seems to have taken a secret pleasure in the burlesque use
of his own initials. W and T appear in Théophile Wagstaff; M and T in
Michael Angelo Titmarsh; W, M, and T in Miss M. T. Wigglesworth, and
in Teresa MacWhirter, who lived at Whistlebinkie.

of the development of burlesque in the English theatre in the past three and a half centuries together with the names of the principal authors who have created the canonical jokes of the burlesque tradition.

ACADEMIC JARGON	Ben Jonson; Fielding.
ALLITERATIVE DRAMA . . .	Shakespeare.
AUTHOR	Buckingham; Fielding; Sheridan; Beerbohm.
BLANK VERSE	Shakespeare; Buckingham; Fielding; Sheridan; Shaw; Beerbohm; Herbert.
CHIVALRY	Shakespeare; Beaumont.
CLASSICAL DRAMA	Shakespeare; Davenant; Stevens; Planché.
COMIC COUNTRY MAN . . .	Dickens; G. A'Beckett; Leacock.
COMIC NAMES	Fielding (deriving from Swift); Carey; Rhodes; Planché; the Extravaganza writers; Thackeray; Leacock.
DANCE	Buckingham, Colman; Fielding; Rich; Grimaldi; Rowlandson; Gillray; Dickens; Thackeray; Matthews; Music Hall artists.
DETECTIVES	Leacock.
FOOD AND DRINK	An early joke of pantomime (deriving from the commedia dell' arte); Buckingham; Frere; Leacock.
GHOST	Duffett; Gay; Fielding; Frere and Canning; T. Dibdin.
BOMBASTIC HERO	Shakespeare; Buckingham; Fielding; Carey; Sheridan; Rhodes.
DISTRAUGHT HEROINE . . .	Shakespeare; Gay; Fielding; Carey; Sheridan.
HEROIC COUPLET	Beaumont; Davenant; Buckingham; Gay; Fielding; Carey; Rhodes.
	Fielding; Carey; Rhodes.
JOLLY JACK TAR JOKE . . .	Dickens; Aytoun; A'Beckett; Thackeray; Burnand; Gilbert.
MELODRAMA	T. Dibdin; Dickens; Thackeray; Burnand; Gilbert; Leacock.
MURDERS, DUELS, SUICIDES .	Shakespeare; Fielding; Carey; Sheridan; Rhodes.

MYTHOLOGY	Kane O'Hara; Charles Dibdin; Planché; Extravaganza writers.
OPENINGS	Buckingham; Fielding; Sheridan.
OPERA	Estcourt; Leveridge; Gay; Lampe; Carey; Gilbert; Sullivan; Leigh.
PAGEANTS	Shakespeare.
PANTOMIME	Fielding; Carey; Henry J. Byron; Revue and Cabaret artists.
PATRIOTIC JOKE	Sheridan; Gilbert.
PLAGIARISM	Fielding; Sheridan; Shaw; Beerbohm.
POLITICS	Gilbert; Leacock.
POMPOSITY	Ben Jonson; Sheridan.
PRISON SCENE	Gay; Carey; Frere and Canning; Beerbohm.
PROBLEM PLAY	Leacock.
PROCESSIONS	Sheridan; H. Farjeon.
RECOGNITION SCENES, "DARK SECRET" OF BIRTH, and "STRAWBERRY MARKS" . .	Fielding; Sheridan; Morton; Gilbert; Leacock.
ROMANTIC DRAMA . . .	Frere and Canning.
SHAKESPEAREAN HUMOUR . .	Beerbohm.
SHAKESPEAREAN MUSIC . . .	Beerbohm.
SIMILE	Buckingham; Gay; Fielding; Carey; Stevens; Rhodes; Beerbohm.
SENTIMENTAL SONG . . .	Canning.
SPLIT WORD JOKE	Fielding; Sheridan; Rhodes.
STAGE DIRECTIONS	Frere and Canning; Beerbohm.
STAGE EFFECTS	Buckingham; Duffett; Fielding; Sheridan.
THINKING ACTOR	Fielding; Sheridan.
THUNDER & LIGHTNING . .	Buckingham; Duffett; Fielding.
TWO MAN ARMY JOKE . .	Buckingham; Fielding; Sheridan; Rhodes.

Before the London theatre is much older this list will contain a new joke, for the success of Christopher Fry will inevitably encourage less gifted poets. Depend upon it, at the first alarm of a bogus poetic drama, Burlesque will stir upon her throne and call loudly for the ink horn.

BIBLIOGRAPHY

THERE are vast numbers of burlesque plays, but very few books about them. The following brief list includes the most important of these. References to other authorities have been given in the text.

A. THEATRICAL BURLESQUE

1. *The Rehearsal*, by George Villiers, Duke of Buckingham, edited by Montague Summers, Stratford-upon-Avon, 1914.
2. *The Beggar's Opera, its Content, History and Influence*, by William Eben Schultz, Yale University Press, and London, 1923.
3. *The Tragedy of Tragedies or the Life and Death of Tom Thumb the Great*, by Henry Fielding, edited by James T. Hillhouse, Yale University Press, and London, 1918.
4. *The Major Dramas of Richard Brinsley Sheridan*, edited by George Henry Nettleton, Boston, 1906.
5. *Recollections and Reflections*, by James Robinson Planché, London, 1872.
6. *The Oxford Companion to the Theatre*, edited by Phyllis Hartnoll (1951), contains an article by Bernard Sobell on the American meaning of Burlesque.
7. *The History of Henry Fielding*, by Wilbur L. Cross, Yale University Press, and London, 1918, contains full details of the *satirical* and *political* apart from the *burlesque*, points in Fielding's plays.

B. OTHER DEPARTMENTS OF BURLESQUE

1. *Scarron et la genre burlesque*, by Paul Morillot, Paris, 1888.
2. *English Burlesque Poetry 1700–1750*, by Richmond P. Bond, Harvard University Press, and London, 1932.
3. *A Survey of Burlesque and Parody in English*, by George Kitchin, Edinburgh, 1931.
4. *The Novel in Motley*, by Archibald Bolling Shepperson, Harvard University Press, and London, 1936.
5. *Caricature History of the Georges*, by Thomas Wright, London, 1868, first published as *England under the House of Hanover*, London, 1848.
6. *Joseph Andrews* (preface), by Henry Fielding, 1742.
7. *Essays in Satire* (preface), by Ronald Knox, London, 1928.
8. *Memoirs of the Extraordinary Life, Works, and Discoveries of Martinus Scriblerus*, edited by Charles Kerby-Miller, Yale University Press, and London, 1950.

C. THE OBJECTS OF BURLESQUE

1. *The Tale of Terror*, by Edith Birkhead, London, 1921.
2. *Blood and Thunder*, by Maurice Willson Disher, London, 1949.

INDEX